THE STEP BY STEP ART OF
Christmas Crafts

4093
Published in the USA 1996 by JG Press
Distributed by World Publications, Inc.
Copyright © 1995 by CLB Publishing
Godalming, Surrey, UK
All rights reserved
No part of this book may be reproduced or transmitted
in any form or by any means, electronic or mechanical,
including photocopying, recording, or by any information
storage and retrieval system, without permission in
writing from the Publisher.
Printed and bound in Italy
ISBN 1-57215-152-8

The JG Press imprint is a trademark of
JG Press, Inc.
455 Somerset Avenue
North Dighton, MA 02764

THE STEP BY STEP ART OF
Christmas Crafts

JAN EATON

JG
PRESS

Contents

Techniques

The following pages demonstrate clearly and concisely the craft techniques involved in the festive projects presented in the book. They include dried flower arranging, papier mâché and other paper crafts, salt dough modelling, fabric and silk painting as well as embroidery. Before you start any project, carefully read through the instructions for the relevant technique outlined here and practise the methods required.

Ribbon bows

Double-looped bow: *Make 2 ribbon loops on either side of your thumb and forefinger leaving a similar length of hanging ribbon on either side as tails. Cut ribbon and twist one end of a 22 gauge stem wire (page 11) around the middle. Tie ribbon around the middle to cover the wire.* **Single-loop without tails:** *As above but make only one loop and do not make tails*

Swag base

Cut a strip of wire netting 20 cm (8 in) wide. Fill with sphagnum moss, packing tightly since the 'rope' needs to be quite solid. Wrap the netting around the moss and twist the cut wire ends around the netting to secure.

Wiring dried flowers, cinnamon, nuts and cones

When decorating with or arranging dried flowers, it is best to attach the flowers and other material, either singly or in bunches, to lengths of wire, since their own stems are often too thick or brittle. Wiring also helps to create a more solid arrangement. You will need 18 or 22 gauge stem wires, the 18 gauge being the strongest and used if the wire is to be the only support for the bunch.

Take a bunch of dried material and cut stems to the required length – usually 12.5-17.5 cm (5-7 in). Hold stems together tightly at the bottom between thumb and forefinger. Bend a wire about two thirds of the way along its length to form a loop. Place the loop under the bunch and hold in place with the third finger. Firmly twist the longer portion of the wire 5 or 6 times around the bunch, but not too tightly to break the stems. Single flowers, such as roses, are wired in the same way.

Cinnamon sticks are available in a variety of sizes. Roll a bunch together in the hand to make them fit together. Hold the bunch tightly, place a wire around the middle and twist the ends together several times. To wire a walnut, dip the end of a 22 gauge wire into latex-based adhesive, then push into the nut base where the two halves join. Leave to dry. Small and medium-sized cones are wired with 22 gauge wires; larger cones require 18 gauge wires. Loop a wire around the cone close to the base. Twist the ends together tightly. Trim the stems of artificial fruits leaving a short length. Wire in the same way as flower bunches or single flowers.

Wiring a terracotta pot

Place a small piece of dry foam into a pot so that it fits snugly. Thread an 18 gauge wire (see opposite) through the bottom of the pot and between the foam and the side of the pot. The pot can then be wired onto a swag base.

Binding stems

Tightly wind stem binding tape twice around the top of a wire stem or bunch to cover the wire. Hold firmly between thumb and forefinger and with the other hand pull the tape downwards so that it stretches. Turn the stem between thumb and forefinger while continuing to pull the tape downwards so that it twists around the length of wire.

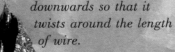

Papier mâché – layered method

1 *Many types of paper can be used to make papier mâché but newspaper is the most versatile. Tear the paper into strips along the grain of the paper. A large, flat surface can be covered with strips 5 cm (2 in) wide but areas with corners or curves may need strips as narrow as 3 mm (¹/8 in). It may be necessary to tear the strips into squares for some models.*

2 *To apply the first layer, thin some PVA medium with a little water in an old container. Brush the solution onto the strips and lay them in the same direction across the mould, overlapping the strips. Use a knife or cocktail stick to press the strips into tight corners. Leave to dry. When not in use, cover the PVA solution with baking (aluminum) foil to prevent it from drying out.*

3 *Brush the PVA solution onto the previous layer before applying further layers. If you can use a different coloured paper for alternate layers, this will help differentiate between layers. Apply each layer at a different angle to the last to help strengthen the model. Strips can extend beyond the edges of a mould and can then be trimmed level with scissors or a craft knife when dry.*

Papier mâché – pulp method

1 *Tear four double sheets of newspaper into pieces approximately 2.5 cm (1 in) square at the largest. Soak the pieces in water for at least 8 hours, then boil in a saucepan for 20 minutes to loosen the fibres. Tip the solution into a sieve and shake out the excess water.*

2 *Use a whisk or blender to blend the paper pieces to a pulp. Empty the pulp into a mixing bowl. Add three tablespoons of PVA medium, one tablespoon of linseed oil and three drips of oil of cloves to help prevent mould forming.*

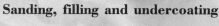

Sanding, filling and undercoating

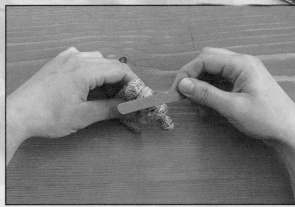

3 Mix together with a spoon, squashing the pulp into a solid lump. Now squeeze the pulp together in your hands. Keep the pulp in an airtight container in the fridge when not in use. As an alternative to making your own pulp, paper pulp available from art and craft stores or suppliers can be mixed with water to produce a versatile, hard-wearing papier mâché pulp.

1 Using fine sandpaper, gently sand away any burrs and obvious unevenness on the model. A nail file is very useful for smaller models or corners.

2 If you want a smooth, level finish to the design, prepare some wood filler according to the manufacturer's instructions. Smear the filler onto the model and set aside to harden. Sand again.

3 A layer of undercoat will prepare the surface for painting. Household undercoat or gesso, available from art stores or suppliers, can be used for this. Apply a second and third coat if the model is to be painted with Indian inks or if it is necessary to even out the surface a little more.

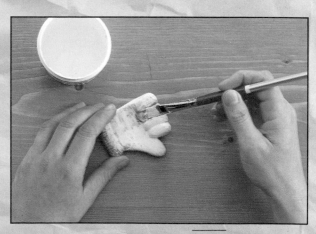

Salt dough

Salt dough is an ideal material with which to model a variety of hanging decorations and its ingredients are probably already at hand in your store cupboard. It can be made in advance and stored in an airtight bag in the fridge or freezer.

You will need: plain flour; salt; water; airtight plastic bags; watercolour paints; varnish.

Fabric painting

1 *Begin by washing, drying and pressing your fabric to remove any dressing or starch. Lay the prepared fabric over the design and secure together with masking tape. Transfer the design on to the fabric using a fine-point textile marker or a sharp HB pencil.*

1 *Mix 3 parts plain flour to 3 parts salt with about 1¹/2 parts water, adding the water gradually. Knead into a flexible dough on a floured board if too sticky. Add a little cooking oil if necessary.*

2 *Roll out to a thickness of about 1 cm (³/8 in). Use pastry or biscuit cutters to cut shapes from the pastry. Cook the shapes in a medium to low-heated oven until they are biscuit hard.*

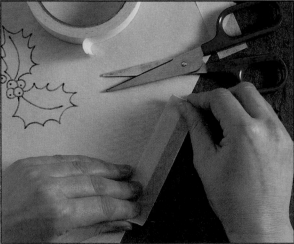

2 *Position the transferred fabric over a large piece of card or layer of newspaper spread on a flat surface and secure firmly in place with strips of masking tape round the edge to prevent it from moving and smudging the wet paint.*

3 *Always stir each pot of paint thoroughly before starting to work with it. Begin by filling in all the small areas of the design. Pour a little paint into a palette or saucer and apply to the fabric with an artist's small paintbrush.*

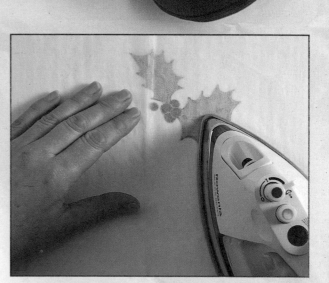

5 *Fill in the outlined shapes with colour using a slightly larger brush, then move on to outline the next group of shapes. You may find it helpful to avoid smudging wet areas by remembering to work from left to right across the design if you are right-handed. For left-handed readers, work from right to left.*

4 *Leave each colour to dry completely before applying the next. When changing colours, wash your brush and palette thoroughly in cold, clean water. Next, again using a small brush, carefully outline a group of large shapes with colour.*

6 *When all painting is complete, allow to dry overnight. To fix the paint, lay a large sheet of white tissue paper or greaseproof paper over the painted areas and press with a hot iron following the manufacturer's instructions.*

Silk painting

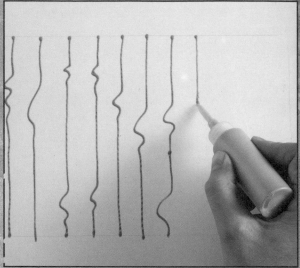

1 *Wash, dry and press the fabric to remove any dressing. Pin the fabric to a silk painting frame or wooden stretcher using three-point silk pins in preference to ordinary drawing pins or staples which will damage the fabric by making large holes in it. The fabric should be held taut across the frame.*

2 *Stir the chosen colour of outliner thoroughly and transfer it to the applicator bottle. Squeeze the applicator gently over a scrap piece of paper until the outliner flows evenly through the nozzle. Apply the outliner to the fabric.*

3 *Allow the outliner to dry completely. Shake or stir the silk paint vigorously. Apply the first colour using a cotton bud. Soak the bud in paint, then press it on to the fabric and allow the paint to flood across the outlined shape.*

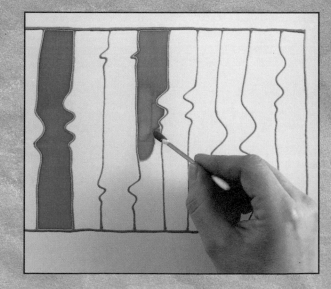

Square box

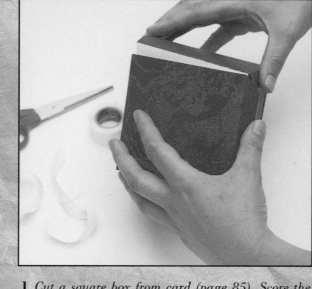

1 *Cut a square box from card (page 85). Score the back along broken lines and bend forward along scored lines. Apply double-sided tape to the tabs on the back of the base tabs and to the right side of the end tab. Stick the base tab under the base.*

2 *Stick the end tab under the opposite end.*

4 *Allow the first colour to dry for several hours, then apply the second colour using a fresh cotton bud. You will soon learn how much paint to apply, but remember that the heavier the coat of paint, the darker the finished result will be.*

5 *Allowing the paint to dry thoroughly between applications, add the remaining colours to the design in the same way as above, discarding and replacing the used cotton bud with a fresh one for each colour.*

6 *Leave to dry for 48 hours. To fix the colours, lay right side down over white tissue paper and press with a hot iron for two minutes. Rinse in cool water to remove surplus paint, allow to dry, then press lightly on the wrong side with a cool iron.*

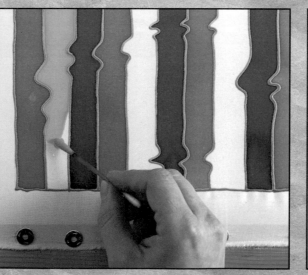

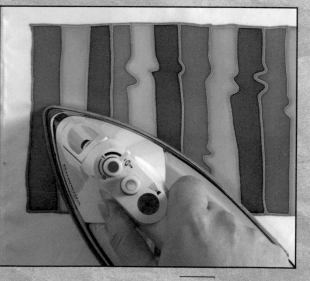

Paper decorations – double layer method

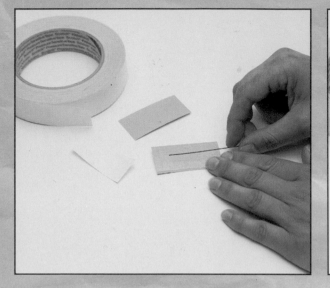

Single layer method

1 *Apply double-sided adhesive tape to paper, remove the backing tape and place a wire along the centre of the strip, extending downwards.*

2 *Starting at one edge, press a second layer of paper on top. Cut out the motif.*

Tape a length of wire to the back of the motif with the wire extending downwards from the shape.

Running Stitch

Running stitch is easy to work and looks good when the stitches are worked to an identical length. Also use as a strengthening stitch round cutwork designs. Work from right to left, picking up the fabric with an in-and-out movement.

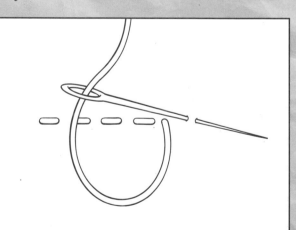

Back Stitch

Back stitch is very versatile - it makes a fine, delicate line of stitching which follows intricate designs well and it is also used to add linear details and outlines to cross stitched designs. When outlining cross stitch, it is often best to use a slightly finer thread for the back stitches – where the cross stitches are worked with three strands of stranded cotton, for example, use two strands for the accompanying back stitches. This prevents the cross stitched design being pulled out of shape.

Work back stitch from right to left, making small, even stitches which are worked forwards and backwards along the row. On plain fabric, keep the stitches small and regular so the line looks like machine stitching. On evenweave fabric, make each stitch cover the same number of fabric threads for woven blocks as each cross stitch.

Blanket Stitch

Blanket stitch is worked in the same way as buttonhole stitch (right), but here the stitches are spaced out evenly along the row. The stitch has a long history and the name comes from its traditional use as a finishing stitch for the edges of woven blankets. Today, it is used in appliqué and also as a decorative stitch in its own right.

Work blanket stitch from left to right, pulling the needle through the fabric over the top of the working thread to make a looped edge. Space the stitches evenly along the row or, to create a more decorative effect, change the length of the upright stitches to make them alternately long and short, or add a French knot (page 20) worked in a contrasting colour to the top of each upright.

Buttonhole Stitch

Buttonhole stitch, as well as being used as a decorative free embroidery stitch, makes a durable finish along a raw fabric edge. Although knotted variations such as tailor's buttonhole stitch are more hardwearing when working garment buttonholes, ordinary buttonhole stitch is perfect for cutwork, in which areas of the fabric are cut away to form an intricate design. The edges of the design are first strengthened with rows of running stitch (left) before the buttonhole stitches are worked. A flat, untwisted embroidery thread, such as stranded cotton, will give a closer finish than a rounded, twisted thread. Work from left to right, pulling the needle through the fabric over the top of the working thread. Position the stitches close together so that no fabric is visible.

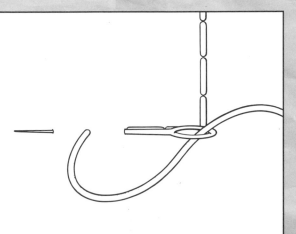
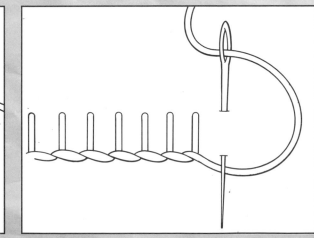
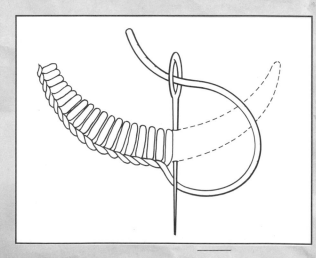

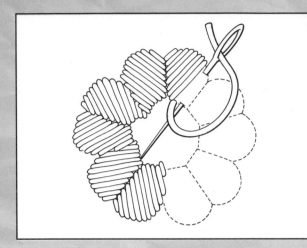

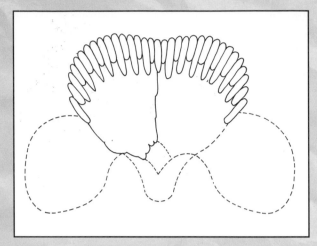

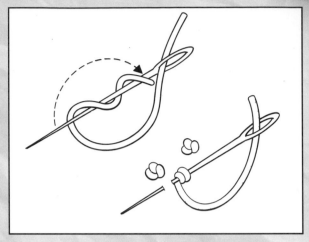

Satin Stitch

Work satin stitches in any direction as the changes of direction will create the effect of light and shade over the embroidered area. You can work the individual stitches of any length, but long stitches will tend to become loose and untidy, so you may need to split up large shapes into smaller, more manageable areas or work them in long and short stitch (right) for a similar, smoothly-stitched effect. Work satin stitch on fabric stretched in an embroidery hoop or frame to prevent puckering.

To work, carry the thread right across the shape to be filled and then return it underneath the fabric close to the point where the needle emerged. Position the stitches close together so they lie evenly and make a neat edge around the shape.

Long and Short Stitch

Long and short stitch is worked in a similar way to satin stitch (left), and gets its name from the long and short stitches used on the first row. A regular outline is created by the first row, then the inner rows produce an irregular line which allows colours to blend gradually into one another without a strongly defined line. Work long and short stitch in one colour to fill areas which are too large to be filled by ordinary satin stitch. Work the first row in alternately long and short satin stitches, following the contours of the shape and arranging the stitches closely together so that no fabric is visible. On the next journey, fit satin stitches of equal length into the spaces left on the first row. Continue until the shape is filled.

French Knot

French knots add splashes of colour and texture to a design. Use any type of embroidery thread, but remember that the weight of your thread will determine the size of the finished knot. French knots are quite tricky to work at first and you will need to practise them in order to work the knots neatly.

To work a French knot, bring the thread through the fabric and hold it taut with the left hand. Twist the needle round the thread two or three times and then tighten the twists. Still holding the thread in the left hand, turn the needle round and insert it in the fabric at the point where it originally emerged. Pull the needle and thread through the twists to the back of the fabric.

Cross Stitch

The top diagonal stitches in cross stitch designs should always slant from bottom left to top right. Work details and individual stitches by the method shown in the first two diagrams completing each cross before proceeding to the next. To cover large areas, work each row of stitches over two journeys. Work a row of diagonal stitches from right to left, as shown in the third diagram, then complete the crosses with a second row of stitches worked in the opposite direction.

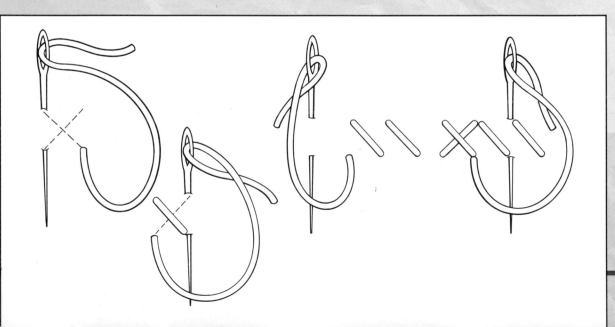

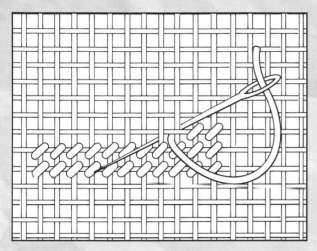

Tent Stitch

Tent stitch is a small, diagonal stitch which can be used for working designs from a chart (Needlepoint tree decorations, page 30) or for a design drawn directly on to the canvas (Floral pictures, page 62). The designs in this book are all worked on plastic canvas which eliminates tent stitch's ability to distort woven threads, so this stitch can be worked in horizontal rows, rather than by the more time-consuming diagonal method. Work in rows, taking a small stitch on the front of the canvas and a longer one on the reverse.

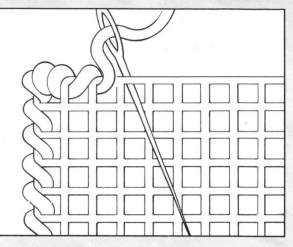

Double Leviathan Stitch

This stitch is used on canvas and produces a pattern of highly raised, square blocks made up of 8 overlapping stitches. The stitch is quite easy to work once you have practised the stitch sequence a few times. When working double leviathan stitch and tent stitch (above) together on the same piece, work the leviathan stitches first, then fill in round the edges with tent stitches. Begin by working a large individual cross stitch (left) over a square of 4 canvas threads. Then work a series of crossing stitches over the top of the original stitch, following the sequence shown, finishing with an upright cross stitch. Keep the tension of the overlapping stitches even and take care not to pull the thread tightly to avoid snapping the plastic canvas threads.

Overcast Stitch

Use to neaten single edges of plastic canvas and to join two pieces together. Plastic canvas does not fray, so do not allow turnings — align edges and stitch together. Work from left to right, taking one stitch through each hole, except at corners, where 3 stitches are made into the corner hole.

Hemming Stitch

Secure hems by hand in preference to machine for a neater look, although a machine-stitched hem will be more hardwearing. Turn up the hem and secure with pins or tacking stitches. Work from right to left, taking tiny stitches through both the fabric and the folded hem edge.

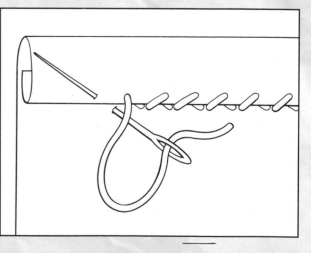

Decorations

Adorn your home at Christmas time with 'alternative' decorative trees, or ornament a traditional tree with luxurious hand-sewn and embroidered decorations; deck your mantelpiece, wall or door with sumptuous garlands and wreaths, and crown your festive table with stunning swags and centrepieces.

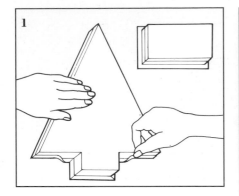

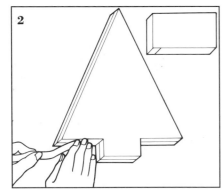

Following the diagram on page 88, cut 2 trees from 5 mm (¹/4 in) thick foam board and 2 rectangles for the base 13 x 7 cm (5 x 2³/4 in). Glue the tree pieces together, then the base pieces, using spray glue to make one tree. For the partridge and dove trees, apply green or gold paper to both sides of the trees and the bases with spray glue.

1 Cut off excess paper leaving a 6 mm (¹/4 in) allowance. Wrap the allowance around the sides of the trees and the bases, snipping the corners to fit.

2 Apply double-sided adhesive tape to the back of a piece of the same paper you have used to cover the trees and cut strips 1 cm (³/8 in) wide. Apply to the sides of the trees, joining the strips if necessary.

Three unusual and stylish Christmas trees. Make decorations of your own design to hang on the map pins. The bauble tree could be covered with purple metallic crêpe paper, as a vampish alternative, and teamed with silver baubles or other decorations of your choice.

3 *To cover the front of the bauble tree and the top of the base, scrunch metallic green crêpe paper between your fingers and glue to the tree and base. Cut off the excess paper leaving a 6 mm (¼ in) allowance. Glue the allowance to the sides of the foam board.*

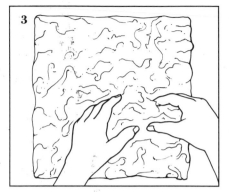

4 *Cover the tree back and underside of the bauble tree base in the same way as the green and gold trees. Neaten the sides in the same way. Glue the trees centrally onto their bases.*

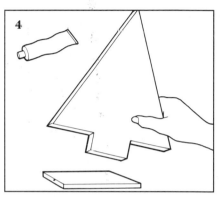

5 *Push map pins into the front side of the trees at intervals. Paint the pin heads to colour coordinate if you wish.*

6 *Cut a partridge and several pears from gold card or doves from white card using the templates on page 88. Attach a loop of gold thread to the back of each decoration. Hang the shapes on the map pins by the loops. Hang miniature glossy baubles on the bauble tree and add a star decoration to the top of the tree.*

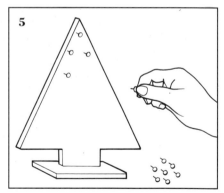

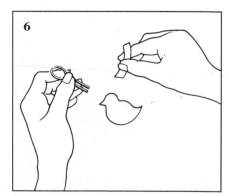

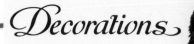

◀ As an unusual alternative to the traditional Christmas tree, why not make an elegant moss topiary which can be decorated with miniature baubles. Follow the instructions on the opposite page to make the topiary base, but use a foam cone in place of the rectangular pieces of foam. Trim the brown root part from clumps of bung moss. Squeeze glue from a glue gun onto the underside of the moss keeping your fingers well away from the hot glue. Place the moss clumps onto the cone as close together as possible. Glue baubles onto the moss to complete. You could make 2 matching trees to stand either side of a fireplace.

▶ A chunky topiary of plump, glossy artificial fruits which would make a colourful and original table centrepiece for a festive feast.

You will need:
A branch approximately
7.5 cm (3 in) in diameter,
20 cm (8 in) in length
Small artificial fruits such as
redcurrants, blackcurrants
and grapes
Large artificial fruits such as
apples and plums
Artificial leaves

1

2

1 *Fill a bowl three-quarters full with nylon-reinforced or quick-drying plaster. Set the branch in the centre of the bowl. When the plaster is dry, cover the top with moss.*

2 *Trim the ends of rectangular pieces of foam at an angle and glue together to form a large oblong with curved ends. Cut a 5 cm (2 in) deep hole in the base of the foam approximately the same diameter as the branch. Squeeze some glue from a glue gun into the hole and push the foam onto the branch. Trim stems of fruits to leave short lengths. Wire large fruits singly with 18 gauge wires; smaller fruits in small and large bunches (page 11). Cover all wires with stem binding tape (page 11). Position fruits close together in the foam. Intersperse artificial leaves.*

Decorations

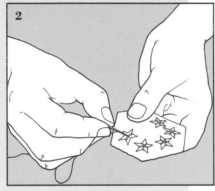

▶ *Indian-inspired beadwork and
brightly coloured felt shapes
combine to make a set of unusual
tree decorations which, with care,
will give pleasure for many years
to come.*

1 *Trace off the templates on
pages 80-81 and transfer to thin
card. Cut out the templates with
a craft knife. To make the front
pieces, place the templates on the
felt and draw round the outside
with a felt pen and cut out the
shapes. You will also need to cut
out corresponding back pieces
about 1.5 cm (1/2 in) larger all
round from contrasting colours of
felt. Also cut out a piece of
wadding for each decoration,
slightly smaller than the
front piece.*

2 *Decorate the front pieces with
beads and sequins, using the
photographs as a guide to
spacing. To attach large sequins
with a central hole, use several
straight stitches radiating from
the hole or a single stitch plus a
small bead. Use two strands of
thread in the same colour as the
felt shape when attaching both
beads and sequins.*

3 *To assemble, place a front piece right side up over the corresponding back piece. Slip a piece of wadding between the two and secure with a few pins. Blanket stitch (page 19) round the edge with two strands of matching thread.*

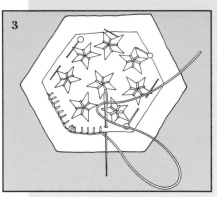

4 *Cut away the surplus felt on the back piece with pinking scissors to make a decorative edge. Stitch a bell or earring shape to the bottom of the decoration, then thread a short length of gold cord through the large needle and insert it through the top to make a hanging loop.*

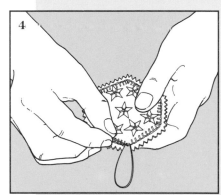

Decorations

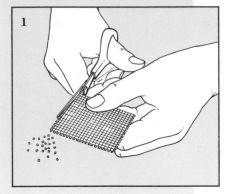

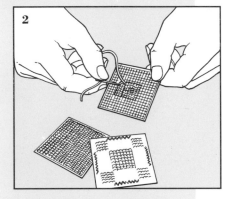

1 *Cut out the squares of canvas, making sure that each one is exactly the same size, 20 threads square. Carefully trim off any tiny bumps of plastic round each piece so that the outer edge is perfectly smooth.*

2 *Following the charts on page 81, make 12 front pieces by working each design twice, using tent stitch (page 21) and double leviathan stitch (page 21) and leaving one complete thread unworked round each piece. Work 12 plain back pieces in tent stitch, 4 in each thread colour, again leaving the unworked thread.*

You will need:
(to make 12 decorations)
24 5 cm (2 in) squares of 10
mesh plastic canvas (each piece
should be 24 threads square)
1 large hank each of DMC
tapestry wool in white; bright red
7606; green 7344
Tapestry needle size 22
Selection of white, green, red
and gold yarns to make tassels
Piece of thick card
12 cm (5 in) wide
12 gold coloured jump rings
7.20 m (8 yd) narrow
gold ribbon

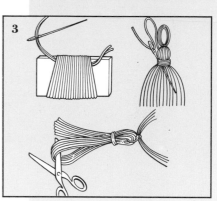

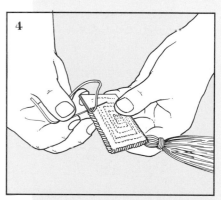

◀ *Squares of plastic canvas
stitched with geometric designs in
green, red and white are finished
with thick, luxurious tassels and
gold ribbon bows to create a set
of elegant tree decorations.*

3 Gather a group of yarns
together and wrap several times
round the card. Cut a 30 cm
(12 in) length of matching yarn
and thread it through the strands
at one end of the card. Holding
both ends of the yarn, remove the
card and tie the ends of yarn
securely. Wrap a second length
of yarn tightly and evenly round
the strands 1.5 cm (¹/₂ in) from
the top and secure the end by
inserting it down through the
tassel. Cut the loops at the
bottom. Make four tassels in
each colour.

4 Stitch a tassel securely to one
corner of the front piece on the
wrong side. Place the front and
back piece together with wrong
sides facing. Using a contrasting
colour of tapestry wool, overcast
the two pieces together, catching
in a jump ring at the corner
opposite the tassel. Finish off the
thread end securely. Repeat for the
remaining pieces. Thread 60 cm
(24 in) of gold ribbon through
the jump rings.

31

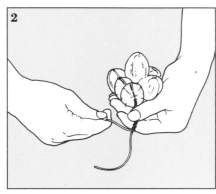

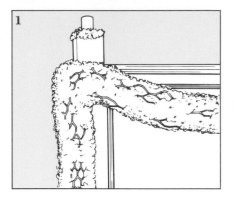

You will need:
Wire netting
Terracotta pots
Bunches of gold grapes
Large cinnamon sticks
Walnuts
Dried red roses
Fir cones, some sprayed gold
Woodland cones
Artificial plums
Lychin and sphagnum moss
Velvet or an alternative
furnishing fabric
Wire-edged ribbon

▶ *Complete this dramatic fireplace display by tying decorative wire-edged ribbon around the cinnamon bundles so that it conceals the wire, and add a large double-looped bow to the centre point of the swag (page 10).*

1 *Make a swag base (page 10) long enough to loop across mantelpiece with a length hanging down either side. Secure in place with nails or by threading wire through back of mantelpiece. Twist fabric loosely around swag beginning in centre and working outwards. Wire in place at ends of swag. Fill pots with foam and wire (page 11). Push wires through swag to netting on far side and twist onto wire.*

2 *Mount nuts onto wire stems (page 11) and wire together in large bunches. Fill pots with walnuts and roses. Wire fruits in groups of 3-4, bunches of grapes singly, cinnamon sticks in bunches and cones (page 11). Wire onto swag, interspersed with clumps of lychin moss.*

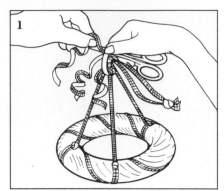

1 *Bind a willow ring with tartan giftwrapping ribbon, applying glue to the ends and pushing them into the willow. Cut 6 1-m (40-in) lengths of tartan ribbon. Tie the free ends of the lengths of ribbon around the ring, dividing it into thirds, extending ribbons 25 cm (10 in) above the knot. Pull the free ends smoothly over the back of a pair of scissors to curl them.*

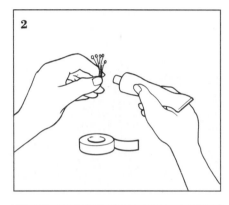

2 *Bunch together about 12 yellow stamen strings and bend in half. Dab with glue close to the fold. When the glue has dried, bind together with floral tape.*

3 *To make a poinsettia flower, use the clematis template on page 88 to cut 6 petals from red paper and to make 2 leaves from green paper following the double layer method on page 18. Bind 3 petals to the stamens with floral tape, then add the remaining 3 between them. Make about 6 or 7 poinsettias and 12-14 leaves.*

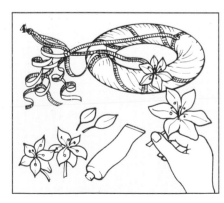

4 *Bind the wire stems of the leaves with floral tape. Dab glue onto the poinsettia wires and push into the ring. Dab leaf stems in the same way and position 2 leaves each side of every flower.*

1 *Cut metallic crêpe paper 150 x 24 cm (60 x 10 in) and join the short ends together on the reverse of the paper with adhesive tape.*

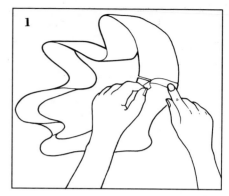

2 *Place a 25 cm (10 in) diameter dry foam ring in the middle of the circle of paper. Staple the long edges of the paper together to enclose the ring, arranging the join under the ring.*

▲ *When hung on a door, this sparkling wreath would signal a suitably festive welcome to party guests.*

3 *Wrap 4 small boxes with foil giftwrap and fasten with giftwrapping ribbon. Bend lengths of wire in half and thread through the ribbon on the underside of the boxes. Thread wire through the rings of glossy baubles in the same way.*

◀ *Surface space is often in short supply during the festive season; therefore suspending a decorated ring from the ceiling exploits a further spacial dimension.*

4 *Arrange the boxes and larger baubles on opposite sides of the ring, pushing the wires into the ring. Make some stars from metallic card using the templates on page 88 and following the single layer method on page 18. Push the wire 'stems' into the ring together with some smaller baubles. Drape a string of beads around the ring, gluing the ends on the underside.*

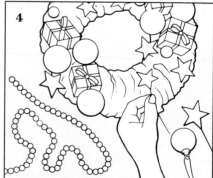

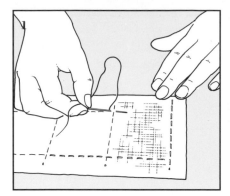

1 *Using tacking stitches, mark out 6 identical divisions measuring 25 fabric blocks square on each green fabric strip. Mark the centre of each square with a couple of tacking stitches.*

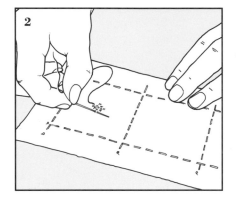

2 *Using the photograph as a guide, work a snowflake motif from the chart (page 81) in cross stitch (page 20) at the centre of each square. Then work the corresponding numbers (page 81) in back stitch (page 19), placing the numbers 2 squares inside the tacked lines. Use 3 strands of thread in the tapestry needle throughout.*

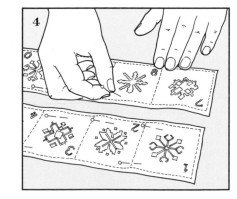

3 *Trim away surplus fabric allowing a margin of 8 blocks outside the tacked lines. Turn under 6 blocks all round, leaving a 2 block margin showing on the right side, and tack in place. Using the gold thread, work back stitch along the lines indicated by the original tacking, removing the tacking stitches as you go. Press lightly on the wrong side.*

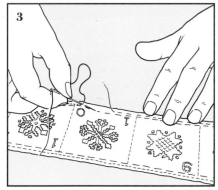

4 *Arrange the strips in the correct sequence on the white fabric, leaving a gap of 8 blocks between the strips. Pin the strips in position. Using the transparent thread, machine stitch along the sides and lower edge of each strip, forming pockets by taking the stitching up to the top edge and back down again when you reach the vertical gold lines dividing the snowflakes.*

You will need:
4 strips 42 x 13 cm (16$^{1}/_{2}$ x 5 in) of green 11 count Aida
50 cm (20 in) square of white 11 count Aida
3 skeins DMC stranded cotton in white
2 spools Balger – #8 Fine Braid in bright gold
36 cm (14 in) square of card
36 cm (14 in) square of thin wadding

Tapestry needle size 24
Sewing needle
Transparent machine thread
Tacking thread in a light colour
Fine string or crochet cotton
Fabric glue
Glass-headed pins
Large needle with long eye
2 small brass rings
24 small gifts
Gold wrapping paper

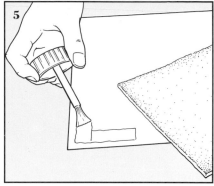

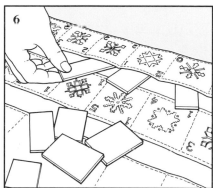

5 Spread fabric glue over one side of the card. Lay the wadding over the card, matching the sides, and gently press in place. Allow the glue to dry thoroughly. Following the instructions on pages 52-53, lace the white fabric over the padded card with string or crochet cotton. Leave a margin of 3 fabric blocks showing round the sides and along the lower edge and 2 blocks along the top edge.

6 Stitch a brass ring securely to the top corners on the back of the calendar. Wrap the gifts neatly with gold paper and tuck a gift into each pocket. Tap two picture pins into the wall to correspond with the rings and hang up the calendar, or stand the calendar on a shelf or piece of furniture.

◀ Wrap 24 presents and open one on each day of December until the big day finally arrives! Tiny notebooks, chocolate bars, puzzles and packs of small coloured pencils make good gifts.

Decorations

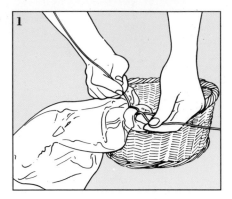

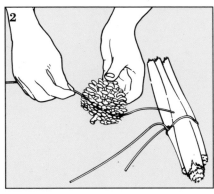

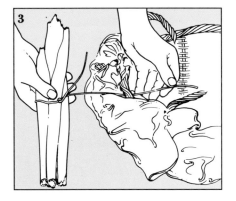

1 *Attach fabric to basket rim at 15 cm (6 in) intervals with 22 gauge wires (page 11).*

2 *Mount cones onto 18 gauge wires (page 11). Spray with gold paint. Wire bunches of cinnamon sticks together (page 11).*

3 *Attach cinnamon bundles and cones to basket rim with wire 'stems'. Trim excess wires. Tie ribbon around each cinnamon bundle to cover wire.*

▼ *If you wish to fill the basket with pot pourri, line the basket with fabric before you begin.*

You will need:
A basket
Gold paint
Large cinnamon sticks
Cones
Fabric
Ribbon

You will need:
A 30 cm (12 in) diameter
foam ring
Bunches of gold grapes
Lavender
Marjoram
Woodland cones
Small dried red roses

Artificial plums
4 candles and candleholders
Wire-edged ribbon
Wire lavender and marjoram in very small bunches with 22 gauge wires and wire woodland cones (page 11). Cover all stems with stem binding tape (page 11).

38

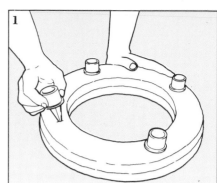

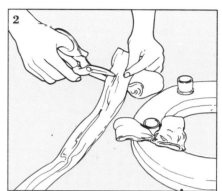

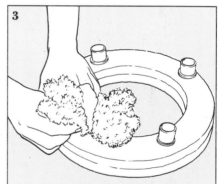

1 *Position candleholders at equal distances around ring, pushing bases into foam.*

2 *Cut ribbon into 8 equal lengths and make single loop bows without tails (page 10). Place 2 bows by each candleholder.*

3 *Mount candles, then position cones. Add lavender, then marjoram and roses. Complete with artificial plums and gold grapes.*

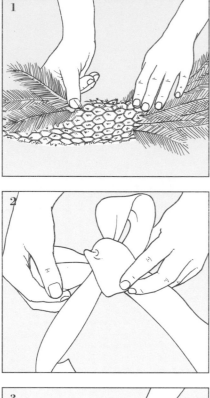

1 *Make a swag base following the instructions on page 10. Cover with evergreen foliage, tucking stems in firmly and working from the centre outwards.*

2 *Make 2 bows from wire-edged ribbon. Wire onto swag.*

3 *Wire baubles at equal intervals along swag.*

1 *Make salt dough following the instructions on page 14. Roll out to about 75 mm (¹/4 in) thick. Cut out Christmas shapes with pastry or biscuit cutters. Pierce a hole at the top of each shape for hanging and at the bottom of bell shapes to add a 'clapper'. Bake the shapes. Paint the pieces, then varnish 5 times to give a high gloss finish.*

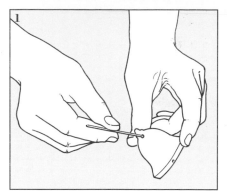

2 *Paint details on the bell shapes with gold paint. Hang shapes on glitter thread, tying the knot just above the hole so that they hang straight. Glue gold bows to the tops of the bells.*

◄ ▲ *Bring a festive air to the buffet table by using Christmas baubles and bows to create a decorative evergreen swag. Alternatively, adorn a fir-clad swag base with glittering salt dough decorations which are so quick and easy to make.*

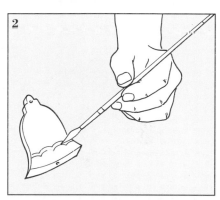

3 *Push a pipecleaner into a bead. Cut the end about 1 cm (³/8 in) above the bead. Glue the end into the hole at the bottom of the bell.*

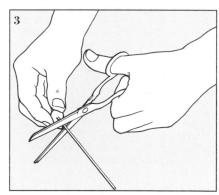

▲ *These painted salt dough decorations in gold, silver and scarlet look equally effective hanging from a simple arrangement of twigs in a jug as on a grand evergreen swag.*

1 *Trace off the napkin motif and scalloped border on page 83 on to paper with the felt pen, repeating the scallop shapes several times as shown to make a border.*

2 *Tape the tracing to a window and secure the square of fabric centrally over the top with strips of masking tape. You should be able to see the traced design through the fabric quite clearly on a bright day - alternatively, use a sheet of glass propped between two dining chairs and direct light upwards from an adjustable table lamp. Draw the design lines on the fabric using the embroidery marker.*

You will need:
45 cm (17³/4 in) square of green linen for each napkin
plus 46 x 33 cm (18 x 13 in) for each tablemat
DMC stranded cotton in white (you will need 3 skeins to stitch one napkin and one tablemat)
Crewel needle size 7
Green sewing cotton
Black felt pen with a fine point
Water-soluble embroidery marker
Masking tape

◄ *Stylish yet casual in apple green and white, this design can also be worked in white thread on white linen napkins to grace a formal dinner table.*

3 *Three strands of thread are used for all the embroidery. Begin by working the plain bars which join two edges of the ivy motifs together - work running stitch (page 18) round the motif until the position for a bar is reached. Strand the thread back and forth 3 times between the motifs, then cover the threads with buttonhole stitch (page 19) and continue the running stitch until the next bar is reached.*

4 *Work branched bars in the same way to join 3 edges of the ivy motifs together, but add a third 'leg' to the stranded threads as shown. Continue working running stitch around the motif. Next, work buttonhole stitch round the ivy shapes, making sure that the looped edge faces outwards. Embroider the leaf veins in back stitch.*

5 *Work 2 rows of running stitch round the scalloped edge, then work buttonhole stitch over the outlines making sure that the looped edge faces outwards. Using small, sharp scissors, cut away the portions of fabric behind the bars. Cut slowly and carefully and take care not to snip into any stitches. Finally, cut away the fabric round the scalloped edge, then rinse in cold water to remove the embroidery marker. Press on the wrong side with a hot iron.*

6 *Transfer the tablemat motif on page 83 to one corner of the fabric rectangle and work the cutwork motif in the same way, making sure that the looped edge of the buttonhole stitches outlines the portions of the fabric to be cut away. Turn and pin a narrow hem round the mat and finish off with 2 rows of machine stitching using matching thread, or hem by hand (page 21). Rinse and press as above.*

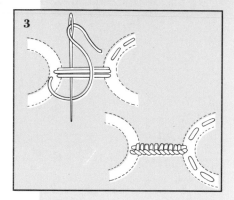

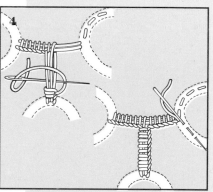

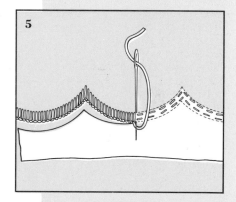

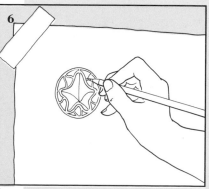

Decorations

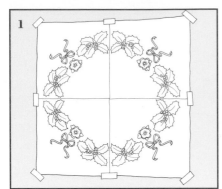

1 *Trace off the design on page 82 4 times using the fine-point felt pen. Stick the 4 tracings together, as shown, to make a large circular design. Secure to a flat surface with strips of masking tape.*

You will need:
Large piece of thin, closely-woven cream cotton fabric, at least 120 cm (48 in) square
Black textile marker with a fine point
Fabric paint in metallic gold, pearly opaque white, grey green

Glass-headed pins
Strips of thick card
Artist's paintbrushes
Black felt pen with permanent ink
Masking tape
Cream sewing thread

▶ *Surround a Christmas centrepiece complete with festive candle with a cream fabric tablecentre decorated with a hand-painted design in soft green, pearly white and gold.*

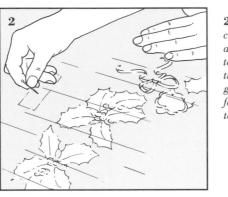

2 *Press the fabric well. Lay it centrally over the traced design and secure with strips of masking tape. To prevent movement round the edges of the design, push fine glass-headed pins through the fabric into the strips of masking tape holding down the tracings.*

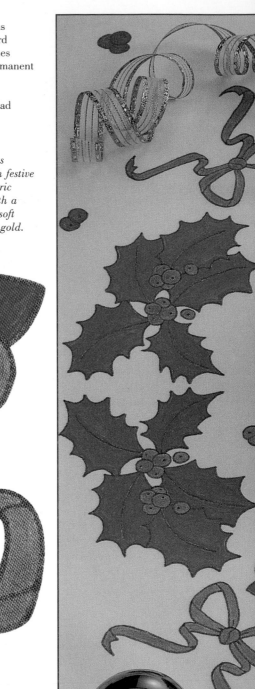

3 *Carefully draw the design on the fabric with the textile marker. Work slowly and carefully, going in a clockwise direction if you are right-handed and anti-clockwise if left-handed to avoid smudging the lines. Allow to dry.*

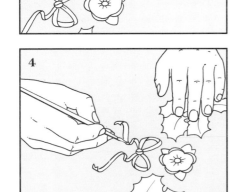

4 *Paint (pages 14-15) the design on the stretched fabric without removing the tracing. Stir the pot of gold fabric paint with a narrow strip of thick card. Using a small brush, fill in the bows, holly berries, flower centres and petal edges with gold paint, working in the same direction as above. Allow to dry – this may take several hours, depending on the temperature of the room.*

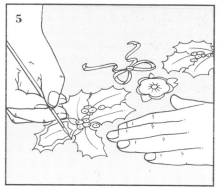

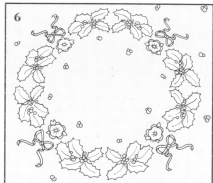

5 *Stirring each pot of paint before application, carefully fill in the flowers with white paint and the leaves with grey green, taking care not to paint over the flower stamens and leaf veins. Make sure you let each colour dry thoroughly before proceeding to the next.*

6 *Finally, use the textile marker to dot tiny groups of holly berries at random over the plain areas of fabric. Fill in the berries with gold paint as above. Fix the painted areas as shown on page 15. Turn a narrow hem round the cloth and secure with a row of machine stitching or hand hemming (page 21) using matching thread.*

Hand-crafted Gifts

Make memorable gifts for family and friends alike - from precious silk scarves to an heirloom cross stitch sampler.

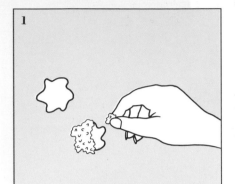

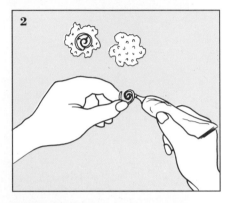

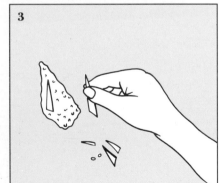

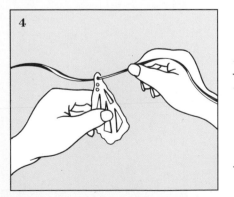

1 *To make the cacti, teapot and coffee pot and the flower-shaped earrings, cut the motifs from thin card using the templates on page 85. Spread with PVA medium, then apply papier mâché pulp following the pulp method on pages 12-13. Pierce holes at the top of the cacti, teapot and coffee pot. Leave to dry.*

2 *Paint the flower earring with craft paint, then coil brass picture hanging wire into a spiral and attach to the flowers with strong glue. Glue clip-on earring fittings to the back. Paint the cacti, teapot and coffee pot with Indian inks. Add details to the teapot and coffee pot with gold Indian ink.*

3 *The heart stickpin, mirrored earrings and pendant are made from papier mâché pulp following the pulp method on pages 12-13. Smash a handbag mirror by wrapping it in kitchen paper towels and hitting it with a hammer. Handling the mirror pieces carefully, dab PVA medium onto the back and press into the pulp. Embed jewellery stones in the same way. Pierce a hole in the point of the heart and in the top of the pendant.*

4 *Leave to dry. Paint earrings with Indian inks, blending the colours together. Apply glitter paint, then glue clip-on earring fittings to the back. Paint the pendant with pearlized paints and thread onto ribbon. Spread PVA medium on the heart and sprinkle with sequin dust. Leave to dry, then shake off any excess. Fix a drop bead to the point with jump rings and a pendant holder. Glue a stickpin to the back.*

5 *Use a plastic bottle as a mould for the bangle and smear with petroleum jelly. Apply 8 layers of papier mâché following the layered method on page 12, wrapping newspaper strips around the mould. When dry, slip the papier mâché off the mould and trim the edge level. Apply 8 more layers around the centre, then add a final layer using giftwrap.*

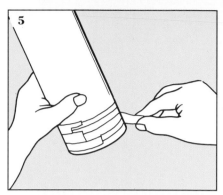

6 *To make the star earrings, cut 2 stars from corrugated card using the template on page 85. Apply 3 layers of papier mâché following the layered method on page 12. Pierce a hole at the dots. Apply pearlized paint, then dab with gold paint using a sponge. Glue a jewellery stone to the centre. Fix a drop bead to the centre bottom of each earring with jump rings threaded through the hole and a pendant holder which, in turn, is threaded through the bead.*

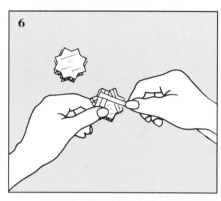

7 *For the necklace, roll papier mâché pulp balls following the pulp method on pages 12-13. Using a thick needle, pierce a hole through each bead and leave to dry. Push beads onto cocktail sticks to paint them. Using a sponge, dab with glossy paint in two different colours. Thread the beads onto a length of strong thread. Fasten each end onto torpedo clasps.*

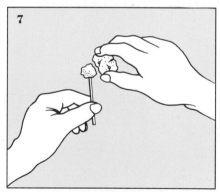

8 *To complete the drop earrings, thread a large jump ring or pendant holder through the hole at the top of each earring, then attach to a small jump ring. Affix to earring wires.*

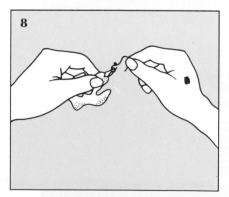

◀ *Here is an exciting collection of papier mâché jewellery that is both simple and fun to make. The techniques used can easily be adapted to create a wide range of designer-style accessories.*

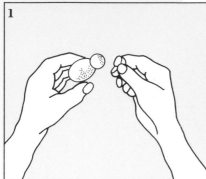

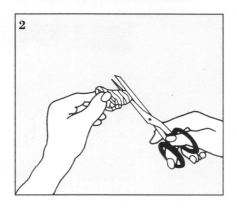

1 For the bumble bee, mould a clay oval for the abdomen and two balls for the thorax and head. Press the thorax to the abdomen. Cut the head in half and press one half onto the thorax.

2 Roll out a piece of clay to a thickness of 6 mm (¹/₄ in). Use the template on page 85 to cut a pair of clay wings. Pat the edges to curve them. Smear clay with petroleum jelly. Following the layered method on page 12, apply 6 layers of papier mâché to the moulds, but not to the wing undersides. Cut a flat oval from the underside of the bee with a craft knife. Remove clay and trim wing edges level. Spread glue on the flat underside of the bee and press onto thick card. Cut away the card around the bee. Sand and undercoat the pieces (page 13). Paint with Indian inks. Glue wings in place and attach a fridge magnet to the bee's underside.

3 For the sunflower, roll out clay to a thickness of 7 mm (⁵/₁₆ in). Use the template on page 88 to cut out a sunflower from the clay. Make indentations along the solid lines with a knife. Pat the cut edges to curve them. Press the centre to flatten a little. Smear the model with petroleum jelly. Apply 6 layers of papier mâché to one side of the model following the layered method on page 12.

4 When dry, remove the clay and trim the edges of the petals. Pierce a hole at either side of the flower. Roll a ball of pulp following the pulp method on pages 12-13. Spread PVA medium onto the sunflower centre. Flatten the ball and press to the centre. Leave to dry. Paint the model. When dry, thread cord through the holes and tie around the neck of a bottle.

▶ Make edible gifts extra special by adding exquisite papier mâché decorations. The bumble bee on the honey jar is a fridge magnet. The cheery sunflower trimming the bottle of olive and sunflower oils can be hung on a wall when the oil has been used up. The jar of preserved fruit decorated with golden pears can be reused to hold keepsakes.

▶ *This charming Christmas table centrepiece of a partridge in a pear tree can easily be adapted to make alternative seasonal trees, for instance a brightly-painted exotic bird crowning a tree of glossy red apples.*

1 Mould small pears or other fruits from papier mâché pulp following the pulp method on pages 12-13. Cut a cocktail stick into short lengths. Dab the ends with PVA medium and insert into the tops of the fruit to form stalks. Leave the fruits to dry. Apply coloured paint, then sponge with gold paint. Cut leaves from gold paper, fold in half then glue to the fruit stalks.

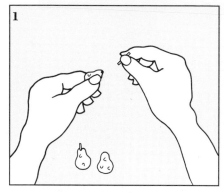

2 To make the tree, cut a slice 1.5 cm (⅝ in) wide from a kitchen paper towel inner tube. Cover with 3 layers of papier mâché following the layered method on page 12. Trim the edges level. Attach the ring to the base of a polystyrene cone with strips of newspaper and PVA medium. Cover the cone with pulp following the pulp method on pages 12-13.

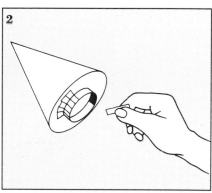

3 Mould some pears and a partridge from pulp. Press the partridge to the top of the cone tree. Cut a small triangle of thick card for the partridge's beak. Dab the end with PVA medium and press to the bird's head. Set the tree and pears aside for approximately 6 hours, then attach the pears to the tree with PVA medium.

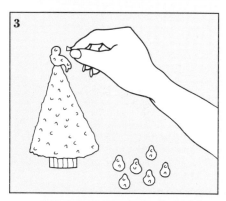

4 When the model is dry, paint the tree base and the partridge's beak with gold paint. Paint the tree, partridge and pears with Indian inks. Using a sponge, dab gold paint over the entire model. Cut tiny leaves from gold paper and fold in half. Open out the leaves and glue to the pears.

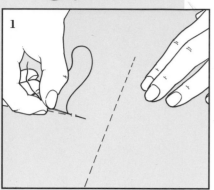

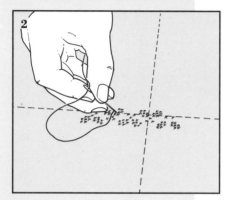

1 *Tack a horizontal and vertical line across the fabric to find the centre. Also find the centre of the chart on page 84 and mark this with a soft pencil (the mark can be erased later). Mount the fabric in an embroidery hoop.*

2 *Work the design in cross stitch (page 20) and back stitch (page 19) from the chart. Use 3 strands of cotton and one strand of gold braid for the cross stitch and 2 strands of cotton for the back stitch. Finally, work French knots in 3 strands of red thread to make the holly berries on top of the puddings, and French knots in 2 strands of grey thread for Santa's eyes.*

You will need:
40 cm (16 in) square of antique white 11 count pearl Aida
DMC stranded cotton in the following colours: 1 skein each of yellow 972; bright red 606; flesh pink 353; yellow green 702, mid green 367; brown 610, chestnut brown 975, golden brown 976; dark grey 3799
2 skeins of bright red 666; mid blue green 911
1 spool Balger – #8 Fine Braid in gold
Tapestry needle size 24
Sewing needle
Tacking thread in a dark colour
Embroidery hoop
32 cm (12 1/2 in) square of thick card
Fine string or crochet cotton
Glass-headed pins
Large needle with long eye

▼▲ *Make the tiny pictures by working individual cross stitch motifs and mounting them in small gold frames.*

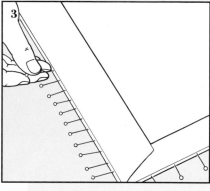

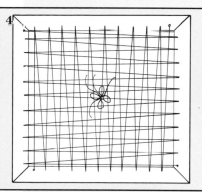

3 When the embroidery is completed, press lightly on the wrong side. Lay it centrally over the card and trim away the surplus fabric round the edge, so the fabric is about 5 cm (2 in) larger than the card. Keeping the fabric grain straight, push glass-headed pins in along the top edge going through the fabric and right into the edge of the card. Repeat along the lower edge, pulling the fabric gently to tighten it, then repeat along the other 2 sides, folding in the corner fabric neatly.

4 Turn the sampler over. Thread a large needle with string, make a firm knot at the end, then lace the string from top to bottom until you reach the centre. If you run out of string before you reach the centre, join another length with a reef knot. Repeat the lacing in the other direction, then pull the string to tighten the fabric and tie in the centre. Repeat along the remaining 2 sides and frame as desired.

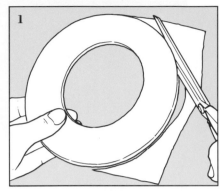

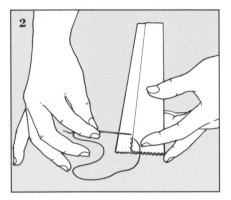

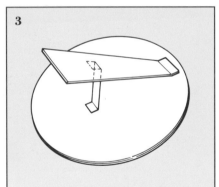

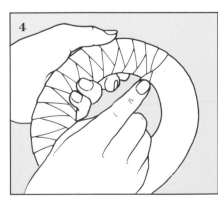

1 Work on a protected work surface and use a sharp craft knife to cut the frames from mounting board. Use the templates on page 87 to cut 2 ovals, cutting out the centre from only one of them. Cut an oval picture stand (page 87) and score along the dotted line. Using strong clear glue, stick the card ring onto 20 x 25 cm (8 x 10 in) of 1 cm (²/5 in) deep wadding. Cut excess wadding from the inner and outer edges of the card.

2 Glue dark green fabric to one side of the other oval, cutting 1 cm (²/5 in) extra all around and smoothing out any bubbles. Snip into the excess 1 cm (²/5 in) and stick over the other side of the card. Cut green fabric 2 cm (³/4 in) longer and twice as wide as the frame stand plus 3 cm (1¹/5 in). Glue the stand onto the fabric centre and stick the excess fabric to the other side of the card. Leave the glue to dry then stitch the fabric edges in place.

3 Apply glue to the top of the frame stand above the scored line. Stick the stand to the fabric side of the covered oval, the corners of the wider end touching the edges. Leave under a heavy weight until dry. From 5.2 m (5 yd 22 in) of 20 mm (³/4 in) wide tartan ribbon cut an 8 cm (3¹/4 in) length. Apply glue to each end and stick one end to the underside of the stand 6 cm (2²/5 in) up from the base. Stick the other end to the oval.

4 Glue one end of the remaining tartan ribbon to the card side of the padded frame. Wrap the ribbon round the frame, making one twist in the ribbon each time it passes over the wadding and overlapping the ribbon edges. Continue until the frame has been completely covered. Trim the end and glue to the card side of the frame.

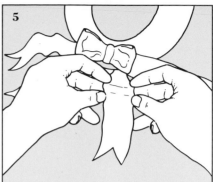

5 *Apply glue to a 1 cm (²/5 in) border around the lower half of the card back. Stick to the frame front. Tie a length of 23 mm (⁹/10 in) wide wire-edged taffeta ribbon in a decorative bow. Shape the bow's tails and glue the bow to the frame.*

1 *Follow steps 1-3 to make a frame using the circular frame templates on page 87. Using 2.5 m (2³/4 yd) of 23 mm (⁹/10 in) wide black taffeta ribbon, cover the front as before but without twisting the ribbon. Glue a 5 mm (¹/5 in) wide double hem to the wrong side of both ends of a 1 m (39 in) length of 39 mm (1¹/2 in) wide print lurex ribbon. Gather the ribbon along one edge using running stitches. Pin the ribbon with the stitched edge around the inner edge of the frame, beginning at the 5 o'clock point. Sew the ribbon edges to the frame and stick to the covered back as before. Fold a loop in the middle of a 15 cm (6 in) length of both 9 mm (²/5 in) wide and 3 mm (¹/10 in) wide gold lurex ribbon. Stick onto the frame, covering the gathered lurex hems.*

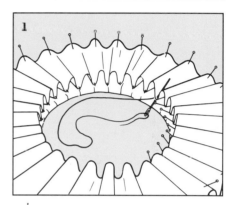

1 *Make a frame following steps 1-3 and using the square frame templates on page 87. Cut a square of green moiré taffeta fabric 2 cm (⁴/5 in) larger than the front frame and apply glue to the wrong side of the excess. Stretch the fabric over the wadding on the front and stick the excess fabric to the back. Cut right into the corners of the fabric covering the aperture. Stick the triangular flaps to the back of the frame.*

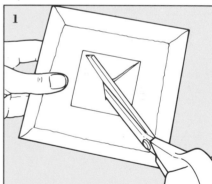

2 *Stick the end of 4 m (4 yd 13 in) of 3 mm (¹/10 in) wide gold and silver lurex ribbon to the back of the frame at one inside corner. Work 3 equal-sized crosses along each side, wrapping the ribbon around the frame at right angles to each end of the crosses. Glue ribbon to the back of the frame. Leaving the upper half free, stick the frame back to the front.*

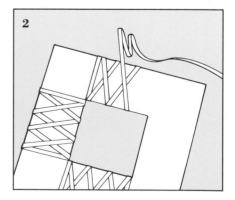

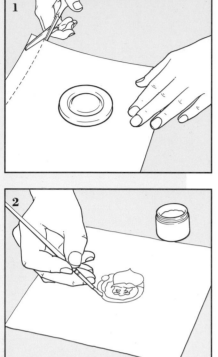

1 Cut the fabric into a large enough square to cover the top of each jar, plus a generous margin to form the frill. Trace off each design from page 89 on to paper using the felt pen and tape to a flat surface. Lay the fabric centrally over the design and secure with masking tape.

2 Trace the design on to the fabric with a sharp HB pencil. Remove the paper design and secure the fabric to a piece of spare card using masking tape. Using the templates as a guide, fill in the flat areas with fabric paint (page 15) and allow to dry. Fix the paint according to the manufacturer's instructions.

◀ *Gifts of homemade preserves and pickles are always welcome at Christmas. Make your gifts extra-special by adding hand-painted fabric covers tied with jaunty ribbon bows.*

You will need:
Assorted jars of chutney, jam, mustard and pickles
Small pieces of thin, closely-woven cream cotton fabric
1 skein of DMC stranded cotton in yellow 973; bright red 666; deep blue 792; mid green 911, deep green 699; dark grey 3799
Fabric paint in metallic white, red, mid green, deep green, royal blue, flesh pink
Artist's small paintbrush
Crewel needle size 8
Narrow red and green satin ribbon
Rubber bands
Pinking scissors
Black fine-point felt pen
HB pencil
Masking tape

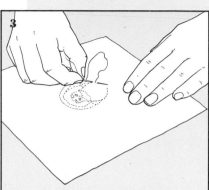

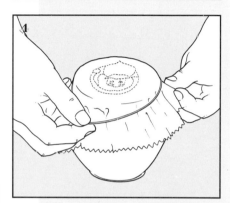

3 *Using the photographs as a colour guide, outline the designs with back stitch (page 19) using 2 strands of thread. Take care to make the stitches small and evenly spaced. Press the finished embroidery lightly on the wrong side.*

4 *Lay a saucer or plate centrally over the finished design and draw round the outside with a sharp pencil. (Do not forget to allow enough fabric to make a deep frill when the cover is fixed over the jar lid.) Cut along the line with pinking scissors, place over the jar lid and secure with a rubber band. Knot a length of ribbon round the jar just below the lid and tie the ends in a bow.*

Hand-crafted Gifts

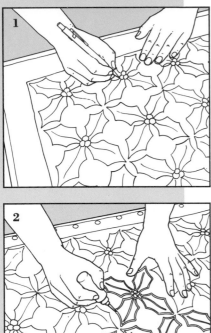

▶ Stylized holly leaf motifs are hand painted in glowing jewel colours on to fine silk fabric to create an unusual scarf design. The second design combines a holly leaf border with flowing, wavy lines outlined with shimmering gold.

1 To make the large square scarf, begin by tracing off the holly motif on page 88, complete with square border. Trace the motif 36 times, then arrange the tracings with the borders meeting to make a design 6 motifs square. Lay this out on a flat surface and secure the silk over the top with masking tape. Draw the design lightly on the silk with a sharp HB pencil, omitting the border squares from between the motifs. Finally, draw a border right round the design.

2 Following the steps for silk painting on pages 16-17, pin the silk to the frame and outline the holly leaves and outer border with gold outliner, working from the centre outwards to avoid smudging. You may like to sign your name in outliner at the edge of the design, close to the border. Allow the outliner to dry thoroughly before proceeding to the next step.

You will need:
Gold outliner
Applicator with fine nib
Large silk painting frame
3-point silk pins
Cotton buds
Sharp HB pencil
Masking tape
Large square scarf:
70 cm (27 1/2 in) square white
Habotai silk
Silk paints in light green, mid green, scarlet, ultramarine
Long scarf:
120 x 48 cm (47 x 19 in) white
Habotai silk
Silk paints in yellow green, dark green, purple, deep pink
Small square scarf:
48 cm (19 in) square white
Habotai silk
Silk paints in light green, mid green, scarlet, ultramarine, purple

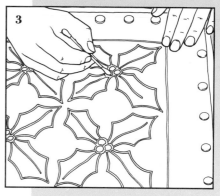

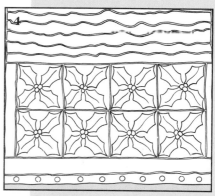

3 *Colour opposite pairs of leaves on each motif with light green paint and a cotton bud. Work from the centre outwards. Allow to dry, then paint the remaining leaves mid green and the berries scarlet. Paint the border area ultramarine. Fix the paints, then turn a narrow hem and secure with hand hemming (page 21) using matching thread.*

4 *For the long scarf, trace off a band of 2 by 4 holly motifs and transfer this to one end of the fabric as above, this time adding the borders round each motif. Outline the motifs and borders with gold. Also draw a gold line right round the scarf just inside the frame, then fill this area with wavy gold lines. Colour in the holly motifs and the stripes. Finish the edge as above. To make the small scarf, draw an outline close to the edge of the fabric, then fill in with wavy lines as for the long scarf. Colour in and finish the edges as above.*

1 *Lay the piece of acetate or card supplied with the box centrally on the square of plastic canvas. Draw round the outside with the felt pen. Mark the centre of the circle with the pen.*

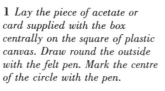

2 *Beginning at the centre and working outwards, embroider the tartan design from the chart on page 90 in tent stitch using 6 strands of thread. Finish the embroidery just inside the drawn line, then cut out along the line. Mount the embroidery in the lid following the manufacturer's instructions.*

1 *Cut the canvas into pieces with sharp scissors and trim off any bumps round the edges. For the scissors case, cut 2 pieces 17 threads by 41 threads (front and back). For the needlecase, cut 2 pieces 29 threads by 41 (front and back) and one piece 4 threads by 41 (spine). For the pincushion, cut 2 pieces 29 threads square (top and base) and 4 pieces 11 threads by 29 (side panels).*

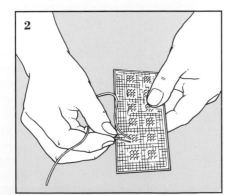

2 *Using the photographs as a guide, embroider the tartan design on the scissors case front and back, the needlecase front, the top of the pincushion and all 4 side panels. Work in tent stitch (page 21) from the chart on page 90 and leave one thread of canvas unworked round each piece. In plain tent stitch, embroider the needlecase back and spine in bright red and the pincushion base in dark green, again leaving the outside thread unworked.*

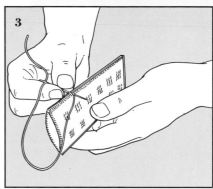

3 *To make the scissors case, overcast (page 21) in dark green along one short edge of each piece. Matching the overcast edges, place the pieces together with wrong sides facing and overcast in dark green round the remaining 3 sides.*

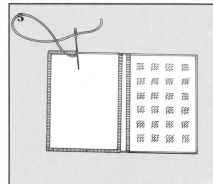

4 *For the pincushion, overcast the side panels to the top, then join the side seams in the same way. Join the remaining edge of 3 side panels to the base, add the stuffing, then join the last seam. Use dark green wool for the overcasting throughout.*

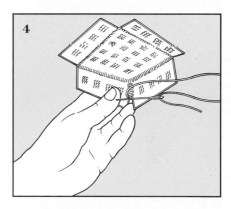

5 *Using dark green wool, overcast the long edges of the needlecase spine to the long edges of the front and back pieces. Overcast the remaining edges with dark green. Cut the piece of lining fabric about 1.5 cm (¹/2 in) larger all round than the needlecase. Place the needlecase right side down on a flat surface and pin the lining to the wrong side, turning in the raw edges. Using matching sewing thread, stitch the lining to the needlecase.*

6 *Using pinking scissors, cut 2 pieces of felt slightly smaller than the needlecase and place centrally over the lining. Turn the needlecase over, so the embroidery is facing you. Thread the tapestry needle with the ribbon and take it through both the spine and 2 felt layers about 2.5 cm (1 in) from one end of the spine. Bring the needle back through all the layers 2.5 cm (1 in) from the other end of the spine. Tie the loose ends in a bow and fold the case in half.*

You will need:
For the trinket boxes
Small, medium and large turned elm boxes from Framecraft (see page 92)
5 cm (2 in), 9 cm (3¹/2 in) and 12 cm (5 in) squares of 14 mesh plastic canvas
Selection of oddments of stranded cotton (5 colours for each box)
Tapestry needle size 24
Black fine-point felt pen with permanent ink

For the sewing set
27 x 34 cm (10³/4 x 13 ¹/2 in) sheet of 10 mesh plastic canvas
DMC tapestry wool in the following colours: 1 skein yellow 7973; 2 skeins orange 7437 and dark green 7389; 3 skeins bright red 7606 and mid green 7346
Tapestry needle size 20
Small piece of lining fabric
2 small pieces of red and green felt
60 cm (24 in) narrow green ribbon
Sewing needle
Matching sewing thread
Polyester toy stuffing
Pinking scissors

Hand-crafted Gifts

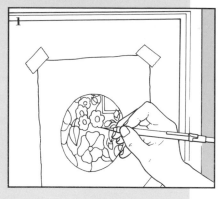

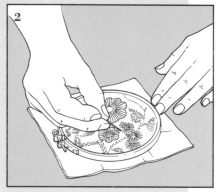

You will need:
14 mesh plastic canvas
Pale yellow silk dupion
DMC stranded cotton in the
following colours: pale yellow
3078 (for needlepoint
background), buttercup yellow
973, deep yellow 972; pale
pinks 604, 605; mid pink 603,
deep pink 602; lavender 211;
purple 208; pale blue 3755, mid
blue 798; yellow green 703;
light blue green 912, mid blue
green 911; deep green 909
Tapestry needle size 22
Crewel needle size 7
Small embroidery hoop
Black fine-point felt pen with
permanent ink
HB pencil
7.5 cm (3 in), 10 cm (4 in) and
15 cm (6 in) diameter frames
(page 92)

1 *For the free embroidery
pictures, trace off the designs on
page 89 and transfer them to the
fabric as shown on pages 42-43,
but use a sharp HB pencil instead
of an embroidery marker. Leave
sufficient space round each motif
to mount the fabric in a hoop.*

2 *Using the photograph as a
colour guide, embroider the
designs using 3 strands of thread
in the crewel needle. Work the
pink flowers, buds and leaves in
long and short stitch (page 20),
flower centres in French knots
(page 20) and leaf veins in back
stitch (page 19). Work the blue
flowers in satin stitch (page 19)
outlined with back stitch, the
stems in back stitch and the
purple lines in running stitch
(page 18). When all the
embroidery is finished, press
lightly on the wrong side and
mount in the frames following the
manufacturer's instructions.*

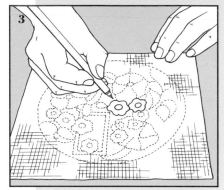

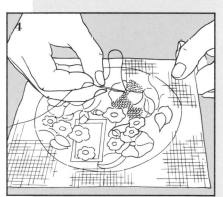

3 For the needlepoint pictures, trace off the designs on page 89 on to paper. Lay the plastic canvas over the tracing and draw over the lines using the black felt pen. To make the work easier to handle, cut away the surplus canvas round the edge, leaving a margin of about 1.5 cm (¹/₂ in) all round.

4 Using 6 strands of thread in the tapestry needle, work the designs in tent stitch (page 21) using the same colours as the free embroidery pictures. Shade the pink petals towards the centre by using darker shades of pink. Work the flowers, leaves and stems first, then fill in the background in pale yellow thread, stopping just inside the outline. Lay the acetate supplied with the frames over the embroidery to check that the background is large enough to fit the frame. Mount in the frames as above.

◀ Make this set of pretty floral pictures as a Christmas gift for a very special friend or relative. Two of the pictures are worked on canvas, while the others are embroidered on pale yellow silk fabric using a variety of free embroidery stitches.

Gift-wrapping and Cards

Wrap up your special Christmas gifts in hand-painted giftwrap with matching tags and cards, or encase them in painted-silk bags, decorative boxes or ribbon-bound packages. Hand-embroider keepsake cards and a traditional stocking for a Christmas to treasure.

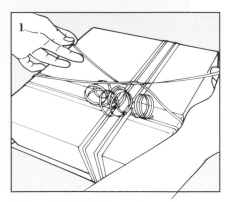

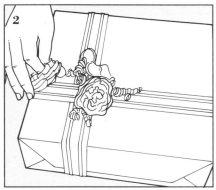

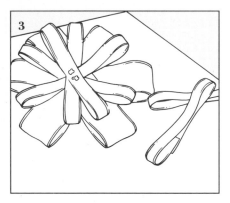

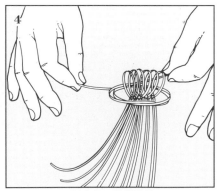

1 Wrap 39 mm (1 1/2 in) wide doubleface satin-edge grosgrain ribbon once around the parcel and fix ends in place at the back with sticky tape. Wrap ribbon around the parcel at right angles to the first length so dividing the top into one small square, one large square and two equal rectangles. Tie narrow foil gift ribbon around the package each side of the grosgrain section of ribbon, knotting it where the wider ribbons cross on top and leaving ends between 20 cm (8 in) and 30 cm (12 in) long.

2 Use strong clear glue to stick three ready-made ribbon roses (or silk/artificial flowers) at the point where the ribbons meet. Leave glue to dry, then pull the narrow foil ribbon over the back of a scissor blade to curl it. Arrange the ribbon coils between the roses.

3 From 111 cm (45 in) of 39 mm (1 1/2 in) wide and 192 cm (78 in) of 15 mm (3/5 in) wide sheer lurex striped ribbon, cut 3 and 6 equal lengths respectively. Form loops by overlapping the ends by 2 cm (3/4 in) and gluing. Flatten the loops with the join underneath and without creasing the folds. Stick the 3 wide loops on top of each other to form a star shape. Then stick the 6 thinner loops together to form another star. Centre and stick the thinner ribbon star on top of the wider ribbon star.

4 Securely knot a loop in the centre of 10 50-cm (20-in) lengths of 3 mm (1/10) wide sheer lurex striped ribbon, leaving 20 cm (8 in) ends to each length. Thread a 50 cm (20 in) length of the same ribbon through each loop and knot at the base of the loops. Wrap the ribbon back around the loops and securely knot at the back of the loops at the base. Cut all ribbon ends at angles to neaten.

5 *Arrange the trailing ribbon ends to spray out from the base of the loops. Stitch the loop knots to the centre of the ribbon star. Wrap the 39 mm (1 1/2 in) wide sheer lurex striped ribbon lengthways and then widthways around the parcel, gluing the ends together on top of the parcel. Glue the star to the parcel over the ribbon ends.*

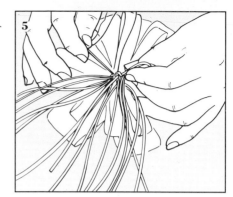

6 *Tie and knot a 60 cm (24 in) length of red narrow foil gift ribbon around an 11 cm (4 1/2 in) deep crêpe paper bag. Alternating red and gold narrow foil gift ribbon, thread and knot 50 cm (20 in) lengths at 1 cm (2/5 in) intervals around the ribbon already secured. The trailing ends should be of equal length. Curl the ribbon ends over a scissor blade.*

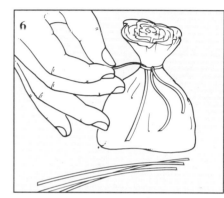

7 *Knot a 40 cm (16 in) length of 15 mm (3/5 in) ribbon around a 15 cm (6 in) deep crêpe paper bag. Fold 6 cm (2 1/2 in) at one end of an 82 cm (33 in) length back on the main length. Continue folding the ribbon back and forth on itself at 10 cm (4 in) intervals in concertina style, ending with a 6 cm (2 1/2 in) end. Stitch through the ribbon layers and ends. Tie the ribbon ends attached to the bag around the centre of the concertina. Stitch or glue a ready-made ribbon rose or an alternative decoration over the knot.*

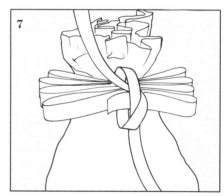

8 *Place the gift in the centre of a large, green crêpe paper square. Gather up the edges and knot together with narrow foil gift ribbon. Trim ends to 2 cm (3/4 in). Using 50 cm (20 in) lengths of 23 mm (9/10 in) wide print lurex ribbon for each bow and spacing them about 3 cm (1 1/4 in) apart, thread the ribbon behind the foil gift ribbon and tie in a neat bow. Trim bow ends and neaten with inverted snips. Using tiny strips of double-sided sticky tape, stick the backs of the bow loops together.*

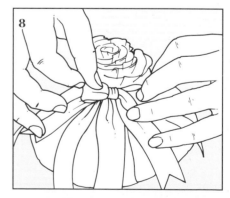

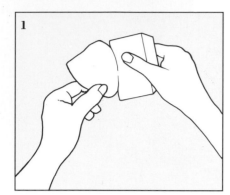

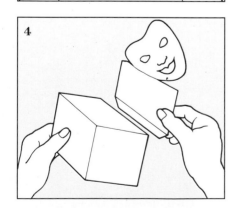

From card covered with marbled paper, make 3 square boxes following the instructions on page 17. Use the templates on page 86 to cut 2 leaf lids from gold card, 2 sun lids from yellow card (outline only – do not cut out features) and 2 mask lids from orange card. Score the right side along the broken and dashed lines.

1 Pull the sun and masks between finger and thumb to curve the card.

2 Spray glue 2 layers of yellow card together. Back with double-sided adhesive tape. Cut out the sun facial features, using the template, and stick in position on the sun.

3 Cut out the comedy face on one mask and the tragedy face on the other. Fold the lids backwards along the broken lines and forwards along the dashed lines.

4 Use double-sided adhesive tape to attach the tabs to the inside upper edge of the box on opposite sides.

▶ All the giftboxes in this glamorous collection are made using the same simple method, then topped with lids of varying designs. Look out for colourful and unusually-patterned papers to cover your own leaf, mask and sun boxes.

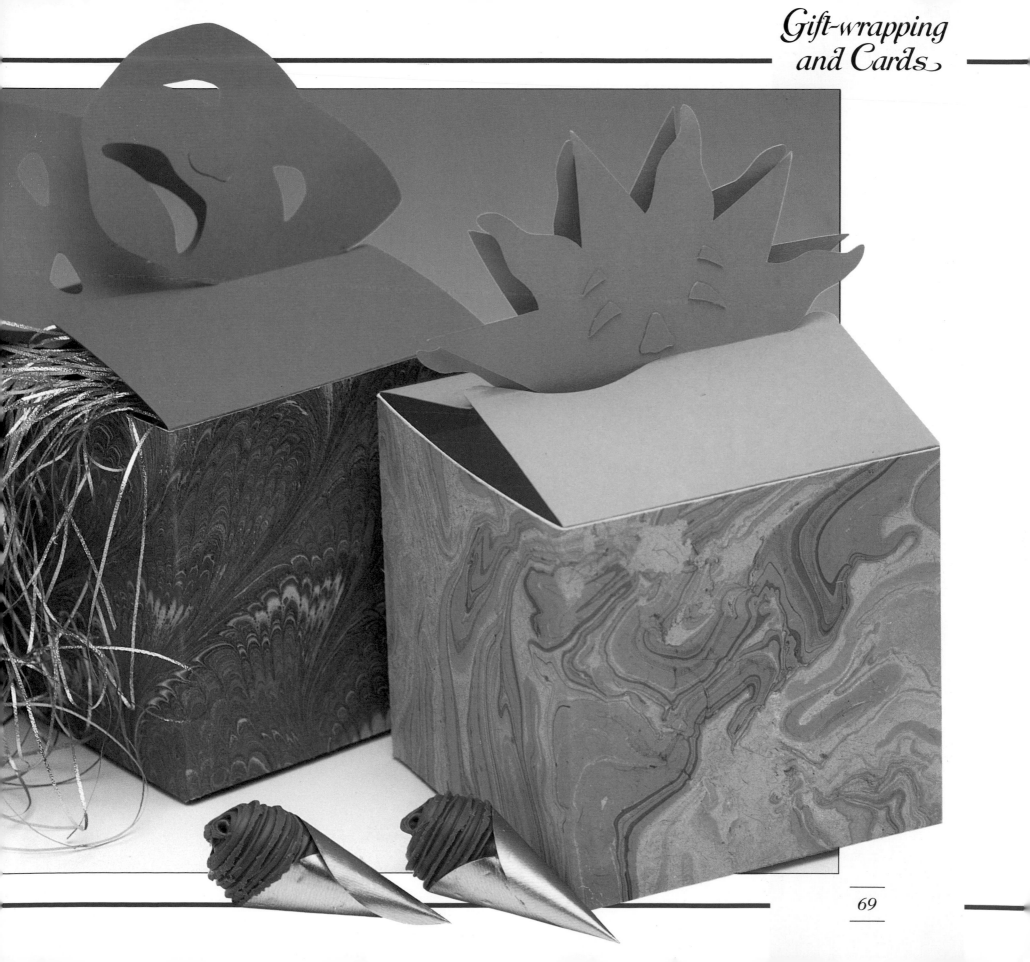

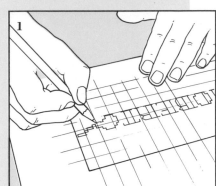

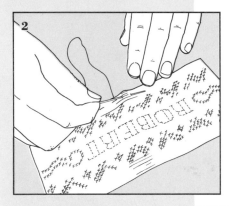

You will need:
13 x 22 cm (5 x 8½ in) antique white 11 count Aida
1 skein of DMC stranded cotton in yellow green 702; red 321; dark green 500
1 spool of Balger – #8 Fine Braid in gold
35 cm x 1 m (14 x 39 in) cotton with a Christmas print, plus the same amount of plain red
Plain or patterned red bias binding
Tapestry needle size 24
Sewing needle
Tacking cotton
Matching sewing thread
Graph paper
Dressmaker's pattern paper

1 *On the graph paper, draw a rectangle enclosing 34 x 76 squares (the number of fabric blocks showing on the finished stocking band). Using the alphabet on page 91, sketch out the desired name along the centre of the rectangle, allowing one block space between each letter.*

Add the scroll pattern at each end of the name, making this longer or shorter as required to fit the rectangle. Also add the holly leaf border at top and bottom of the rectangle in the same way as the chart on page 91. If you need to embroider a very long name, you will have to make the band and the stocking top wider to accommodate the correct number of letters.

2 *Embroider the name, scroll pattern and holly leaf border in cross stitch (page 20) and back stitch (page 19) using 3 strands of cotton and 1 strand of gold braid. Press lightly on the wrong side, then turn under and tack the 2 long edges, leaving a margin of 5 blocks of unworked fabric showing on the right side.*

▲ ▶ *Make a Christmas stocking from fabric with a bright, seasonal print and personalize it with a stylish cross stitched band featuring a name decorated with bands of holly leaves.*

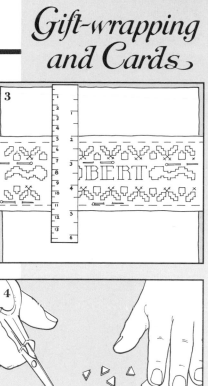

3 Make a paper pattern for the stocking from the template on pages 90-91. Cut out 2 patterned and 2 plain shapes from the fabric. Pin the embroidered band on to the right side of one patterned piece about 5 cm (2 in) from the top, making sure that the toe points to the right. Machine stitch in place close to the edge using cream thread.

4 Sandwich the 2 plain pieces between the right sides of the 2 patterned pieces, raw edges aligning, then machine stitch together close to the edge, leaving the top open. Stitch twice to make a strong seam. Press the seam, cut notches into the seam allowance along the curves, then turn to the right side. Bind the top of the stocking with bias binding, adding a loop for hanging at the back. To make the plain stocking, proceed in the same way, but substitute a piece of patterned fabric for the embroidered band.

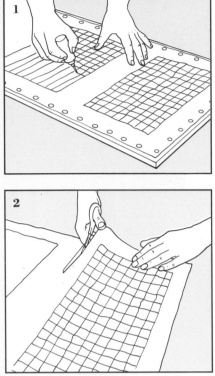

1 Paint several bags at once by stretching a piece of white Habotai silk across a large stretcher or silk painting frame. Draw the outline of each bag on the silk with gold or clear outliner (page 16), allowing about 8 cm (3 in) between each one. Then fill in the rectangles with freehand horizontal and vertical lines of outliner, varying the spacing between the lines to form tartan patterns. Allow outliner to dry.

2 Following the steps showing silk painting on pages 16-17, fill in the tartan patterns with silk paints. Allow to dry for several hours, remove the silk from the frame, then fix with an iron (page 17). Cut out each design leaving a margin of about 1.5 cm (^{1}/2 in) around each one.

◀ *Hand-painted silk fabric backed with a layer of interfacing makes a set of pretty gift bags. Wrap your present in tissue paper before placing in the bag and securing the top with a length of gold cord.*

You will need:
White Habotai silk
Silk painting frame
Gold and clear outliners
Applicator
Silk paints in a range of colours
Lightweight iron-on interfacing
Sewing threads to tone
Gold cord or ribbon
Pinking scissors

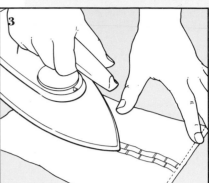

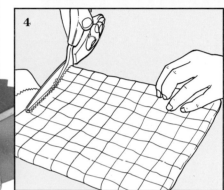

3 Back each piece of painted silk with iron-on interfacing. Fold each piece in half and machine stitch along the side to make a seam. Press the seam open. Fold the bag so the seam falls along the centre back, then machine along the lower edge. Press the seam.

4 Clip off the surplus fabric at the lower corners, then turn the bag to the right side and press. Trim the top of the bag with pinking scissors to make a decorative edge. Wrap the gift in tissue paper and place in the bag. Tie the top of the bag with gold cord or ribbon.

73

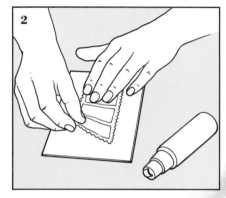

▶ *A simply sponged design in gold paint decorates ordinary brown paper to make tastefully co-ordinating wrapping paper, gift tags and greeting cards.*

1 *Secure a sheet of brown paper to a flat surface with masking tape. Squeeze gold gouache on to a small plate and thin down with water. Dip one side of a makeup sponge into the paint and press on to the paper to make a rectangular mark. Repeat until the paper is covered with patterns. Allow to dry, then wrap parcels and trim with gold ribbon. For the tags, cut squares 6 cm (2 1/4 in) out of the sponged paper and glue on to card. Punch a hole at the top of the tag and thread through with narrow gold ribbon.*

2 *To make the cards, sponge single or triple shapes on to brown paper. Allow to dry and cut round the edge with pinking scissors, leaving a margin of brown paper showing round the sponged shapes. Cut out 20 x 9 cm (8 x 3 1/2 in) and 20 x 15 cm (8 x 6 in) rectangles of gold card, score and fold. Stick the sponged shapes on to the card, thread a length of narrow ribbon along the fold and tie in a bow.*

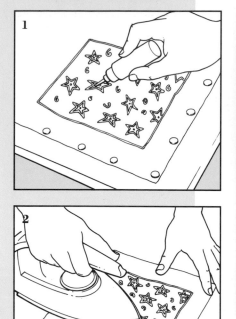

1 Stretch a piece of white Habotai silk across a stretcher or silk painting frame. Draw freehand designs of stars, holly leaves, plum puddings and Christmas trees with gold outliner (page 16). Draw a border round each group of shapes to enclose a background area slightly larger than the aperture of the intended card. Allow the outliner to dry thoroughly.

2 Following the steps showing silk painting on pages 16-17, fill in the shapes and the background areas with silk paints. Allow to dry for several hours, remove the silk from the frame, then fix with an iron (page 17). Cut out each design and mount in a ready-made card as shown on pages 78-79.

You will need:
White Habotai silk
Silk painting frame
Gold outliner
Applicator
Silk paints in a range of colours
Ready-made white or cream
greeting cards

◀ ▶ Ready-cut cards with window mounts are the perfect place to display small pieces of hand-painted silk decorated with a variety of Christmas motifs in strong colours.

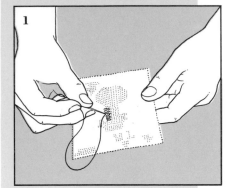

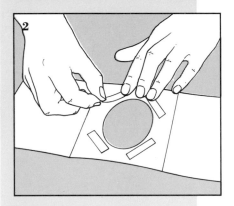

1 *Work each design in cross stitch (page 20) and back stitch (page 19) from the chart. Use 3 strands of coloured threads and 1 strand of gold braid. Lay the design over the aperture in the card and trim away the surplus, allowing a margin of 1.5 cm ($^1/_2$ in) to overlap the card. Place the design right side up on a flat surface.*

2 *On the wrong side of the card, position strips of double-sided adhesive tape around the aperture. Peel off the backing, then position the aperture over the embroidered design and press in place. Again using tape, stick the flap down over the back of the embroidery.*

◄ The Christmas motifs are stitched on perforated paper in exactly the same way as when working on evenweave fabric. Mount the finished embroideries in ready-made greeting cards.

You will need:
Perforated card in red and white
1 skein of DMC stranded cotton in yellow 973; orange 740; bright reds 606, 666; deep red 321; blue 792; mid green 911, deep green 699; dark grey 3799; white
1 spool of Balger – #8 Fine Braid in gold
Tapestry needle size 24
Small ready-made cards in red and white with 8 cm (3 in) deep apertures
Double-sided adhesive tape

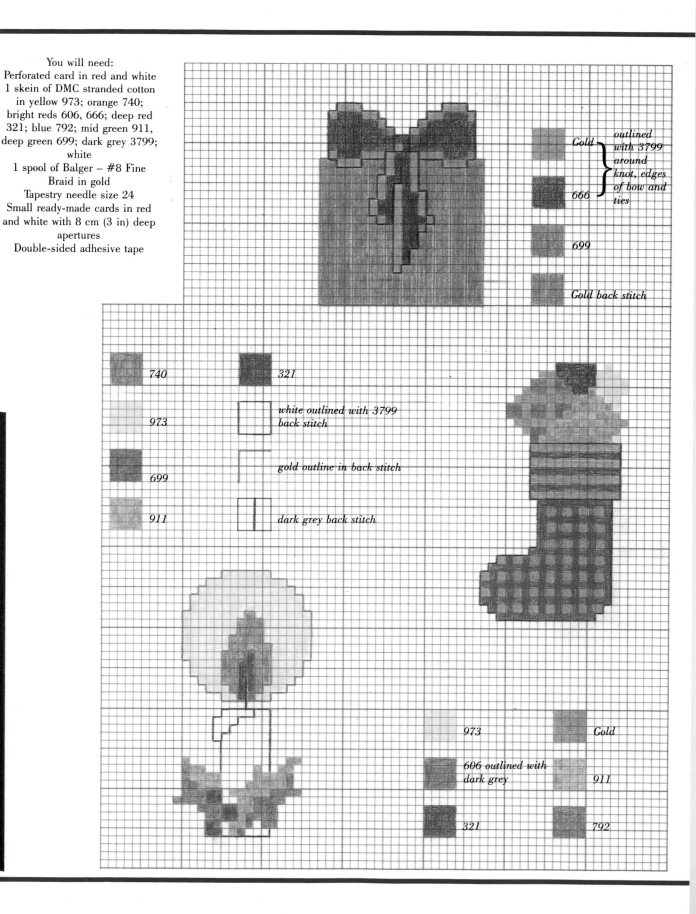

Gold ⎱ outlined with 3799 around knot, edges of bow and ties

666

699

Gold back stitch

740   321

973   white outlined with 3799 back stitch

699   gold outline in back stitch

911   dark grey back stitch

973   Gold

606 outlined with dark grey   911

321   792

Templates, diagrams and charts

The following pages present the templates, diagrams and charts for the projects. The diagrams are constructed from measurements. Use a ruler and set square to draw the pieces onto card to use as a template. It is important to follow either the metric or imperial measurement but not a combination of both.

Some templates are reduced in size, where stated. To enlarge, draw a grid of 1.4 cm ($^9/_{16}$ in) squares. Copy the design square by square using the grid lines as a guide. Alternatively, enlarge templates on a photocopier to 141% (or A4 enlarged to A3). To make a complete pattern for symmetrical shapes, place the pattern on a piece of folded paper matching the 'place to fold' line to the folded edge. Cut out and open the pattern out flat to use.

Embroider one stitch on the fabric for every coloured square shown on the charts.

FELT TREE DECORATIONS
Pages 28-29

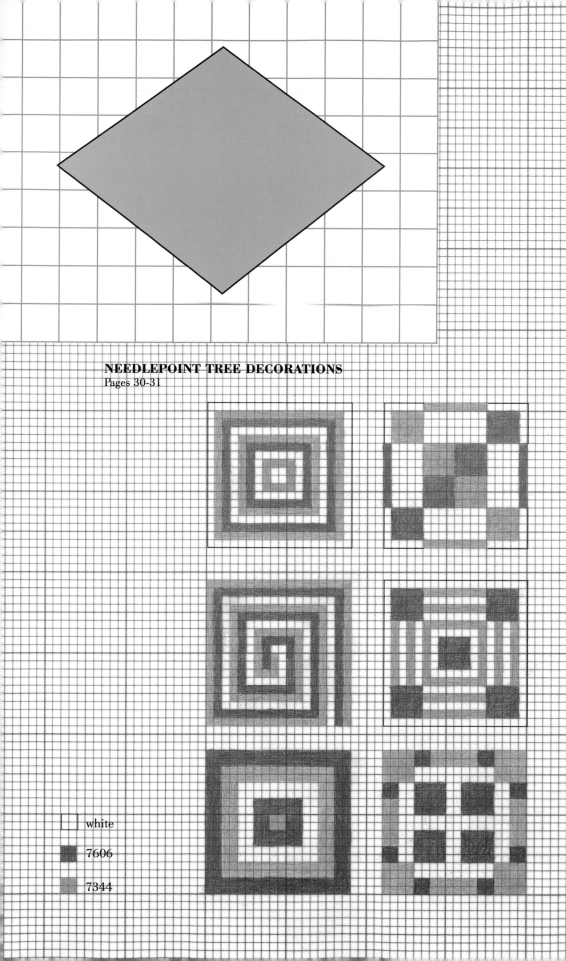

ADVENT CALENDAR
Pages 36-37

NEEDLEPOINT TREE DECORATIONS
Pages 30-31

1234567890

	white
	7606
	7344

81

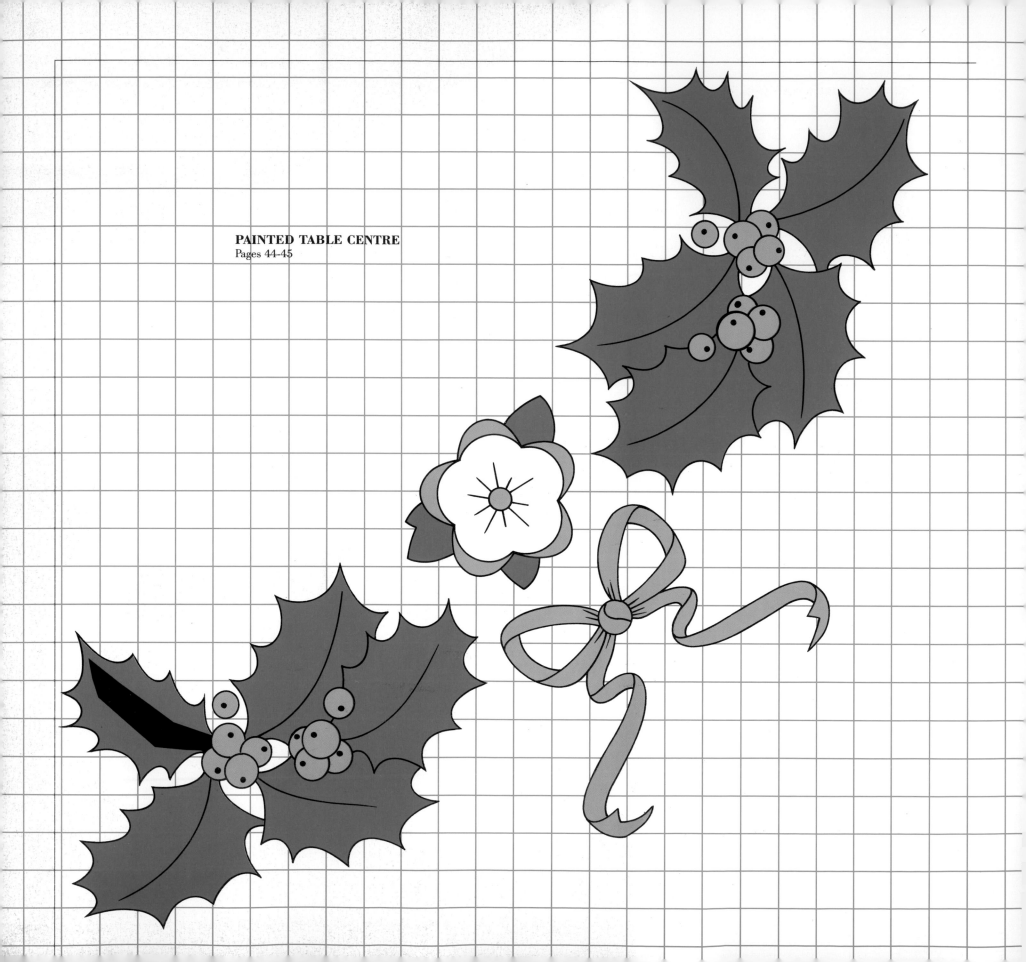

PAINTED TABLE CENTRE
Pages 44-45

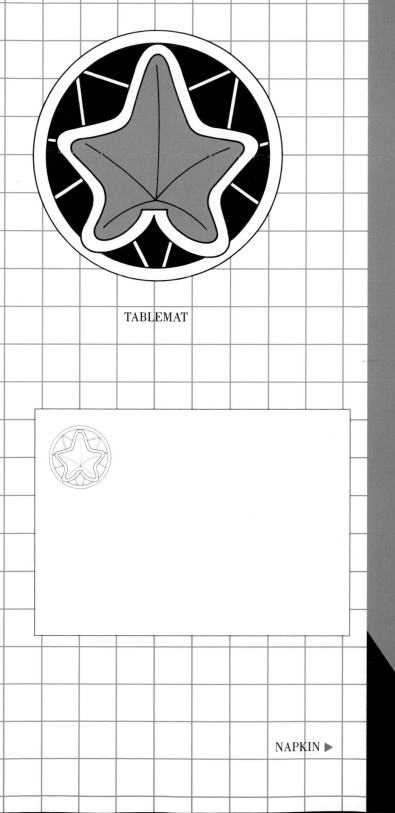

TABLEMAT

NAPKIN ▶

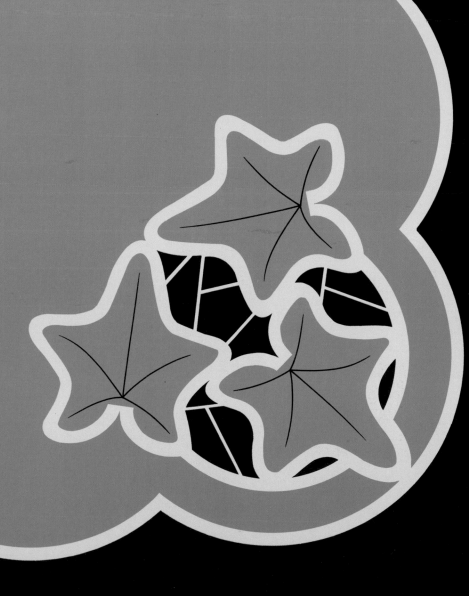

10.2 cm (4 in)   10.2 cm (4 in)   10.2 cm (4 in)   10.2 cm (4 in)   1.5cm (⁵/₈in)

SQUARE BOX
Pages 68-69

END TAB

10.2 cm (4 in)

BASE TAB   BASE TAB   BASE TAB

1.5cm (⁵/₈in)

1.5cm (⁵/₈in)   1.5cm (⁵/₈in)   1.5cm (⁵/₈in)   3 cm (1¹/₄ in)   1.5cm (⁵/₈in)

BASE

10.2 cm (4 in)

**CROSS STITCH
SAMPLER**
Pages 52-53

606

666

911

702

367

Balger fine braid 221

972

353

3799

610

975

976

CACTI

JEWELLERY
Pages 48-49

BUMBLE BEE WING
Page 50

STAR

FLOWER

TEAPOT

COFFEE POT

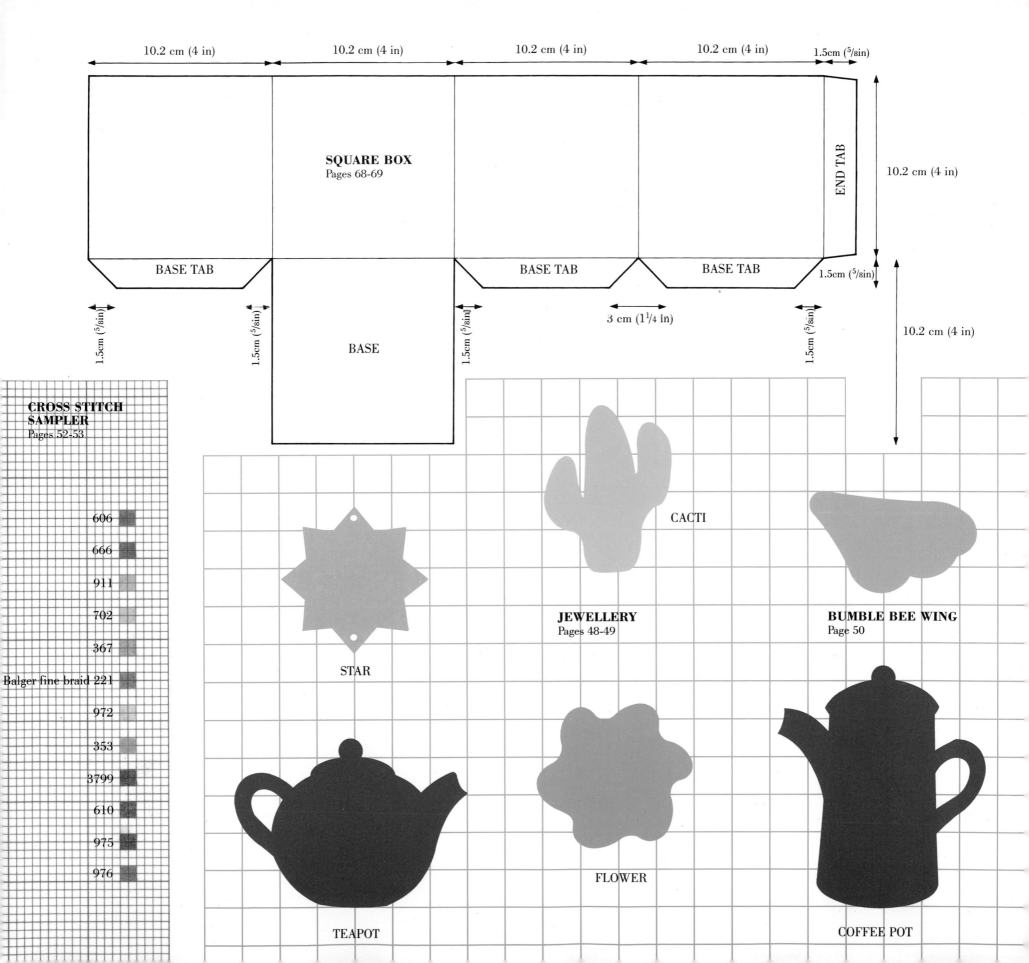

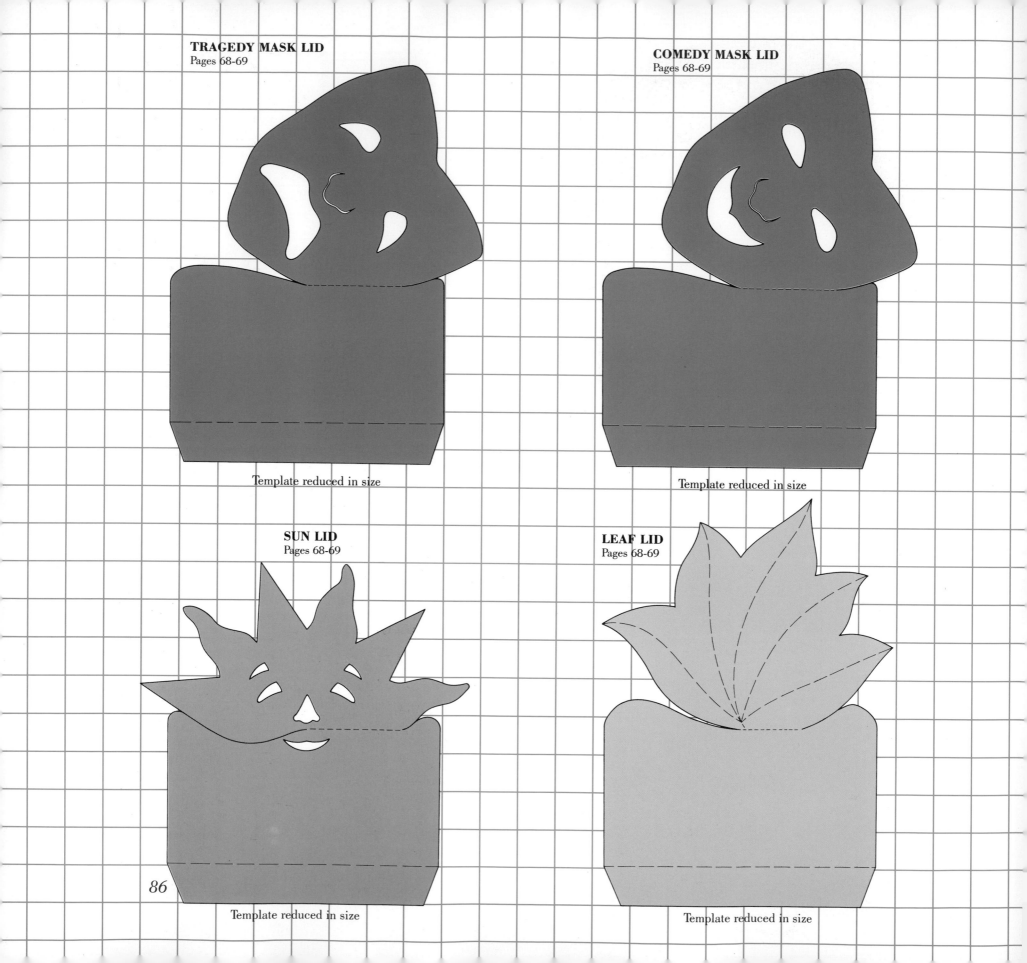

TRAGEDY MASK LID
Pages 68-69

Template reduced in size

COMEDY MASK LID
Pages 68-69

Template reduced in size

SUN LID
Pages 68-69

Template reduced in size

LEAF LID
Pages 68-69

Template reduced in size

86

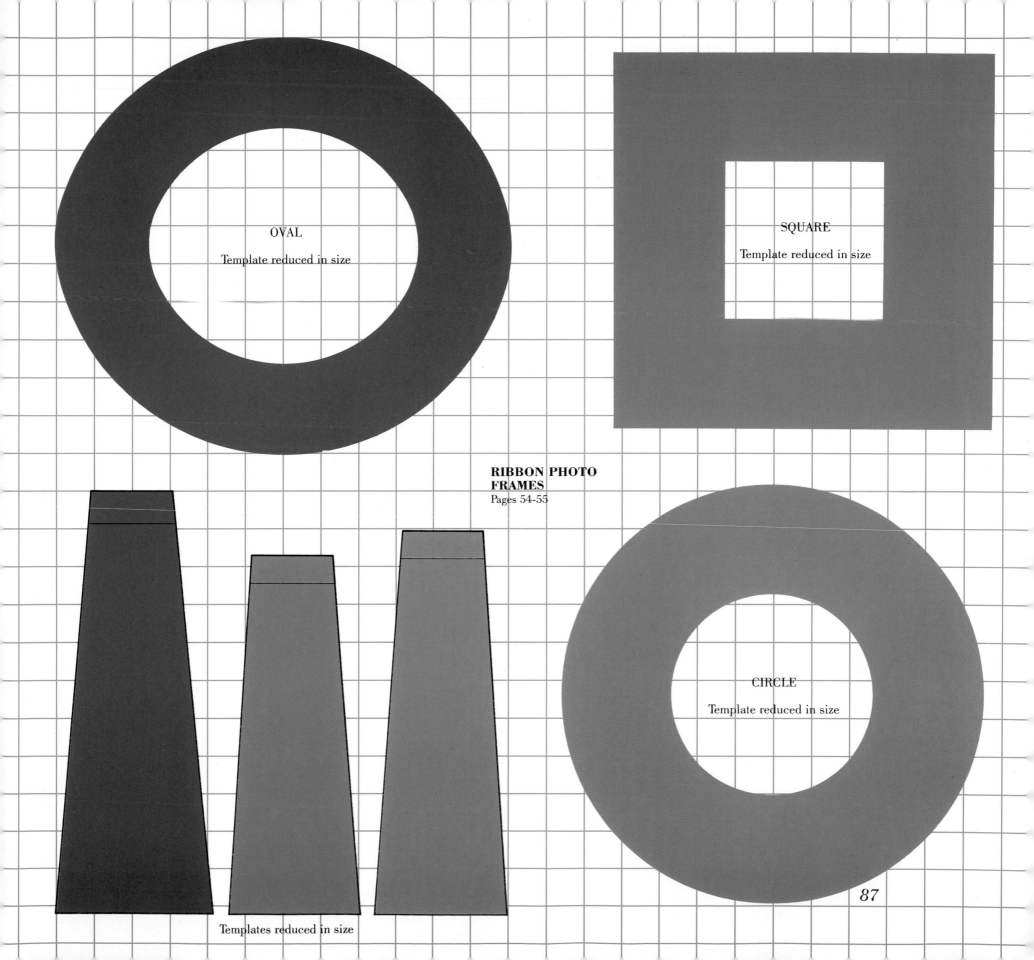

OVAL

Template reduced in size

SQUARE

Template reduced in size

**RIBBON PHOTO
FRAMES**
Pages 54-55

CIRCLE

Template reduced in size

Templates reduced in size

87

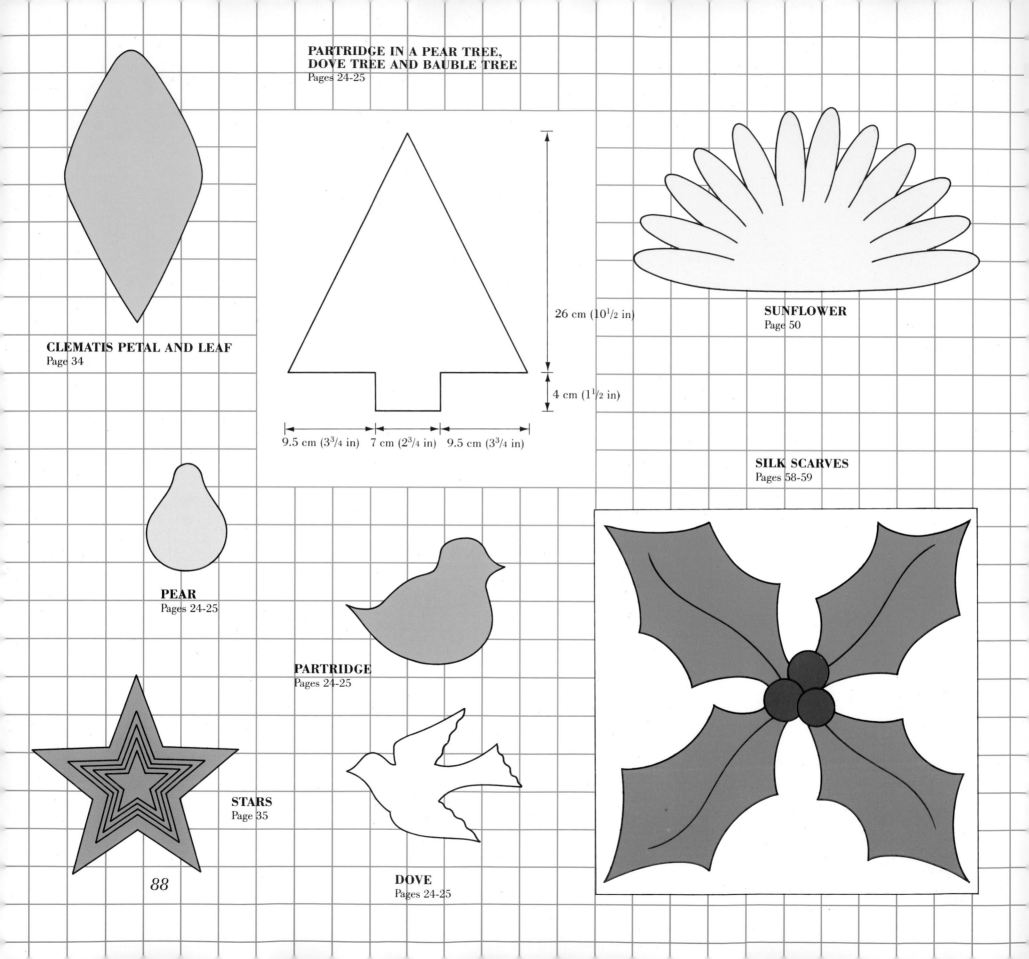

**PARTRIDGE IN A PEAR TREE,
DOVE TREE AND BAUBLE TREE**
Pages 24-25

CLEMATIS PETAL AND LEAF
Page 34

26 cm (10½ in)

4 cm (1½ in)

9.5 cm (3¾ in)   7 cm (2¾ in)   9.5 cm (3¾ in)

SUNFLOWER
Page 50

SILK SCARVES
Pages 58-59

PEAR
Pages 24-25

PARTRIDGE
Pages 24-25

STARS
Page 35

88

DOVE
Pages 24-25

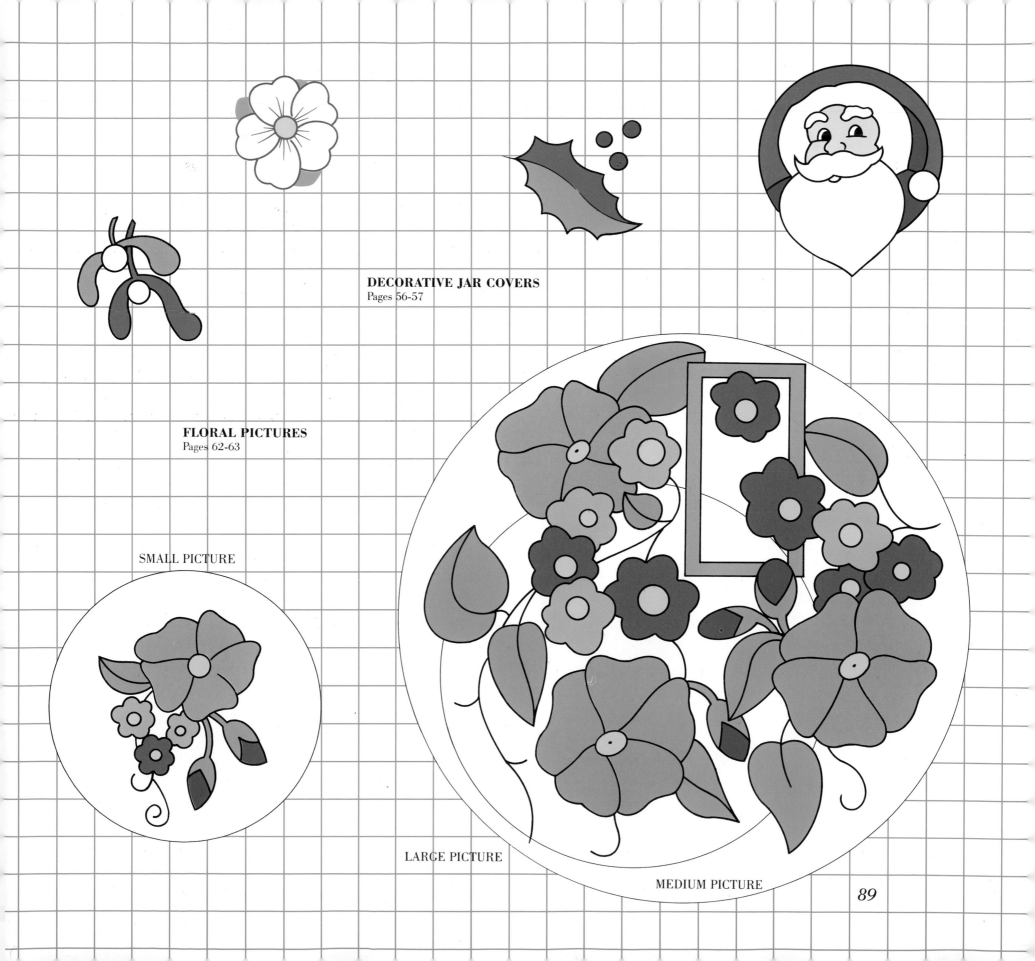

DECORATIVE JAR COVERS
Pages 56-57

FLORAL PICTURES
Pages 62-63

SMALL PICTURE

LARGE PICTURE

MEDIUM PICTURE

89

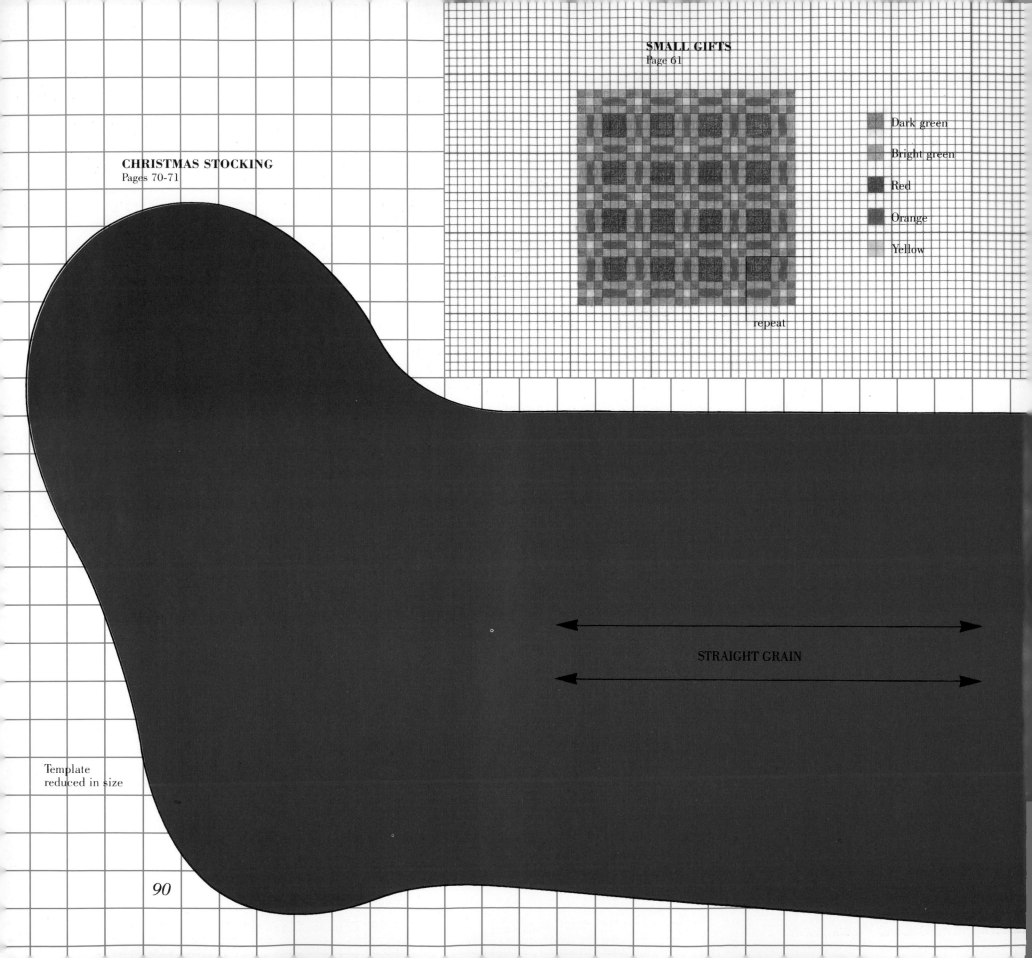

SMALL GIFTS
Page 61

Dark green

Bright green

Red

Orange

Yellow

repeat

CHRISTMAS STOCKING
Pages 70-71

STRAIGHT GRAIN

Template
reduced in size

90

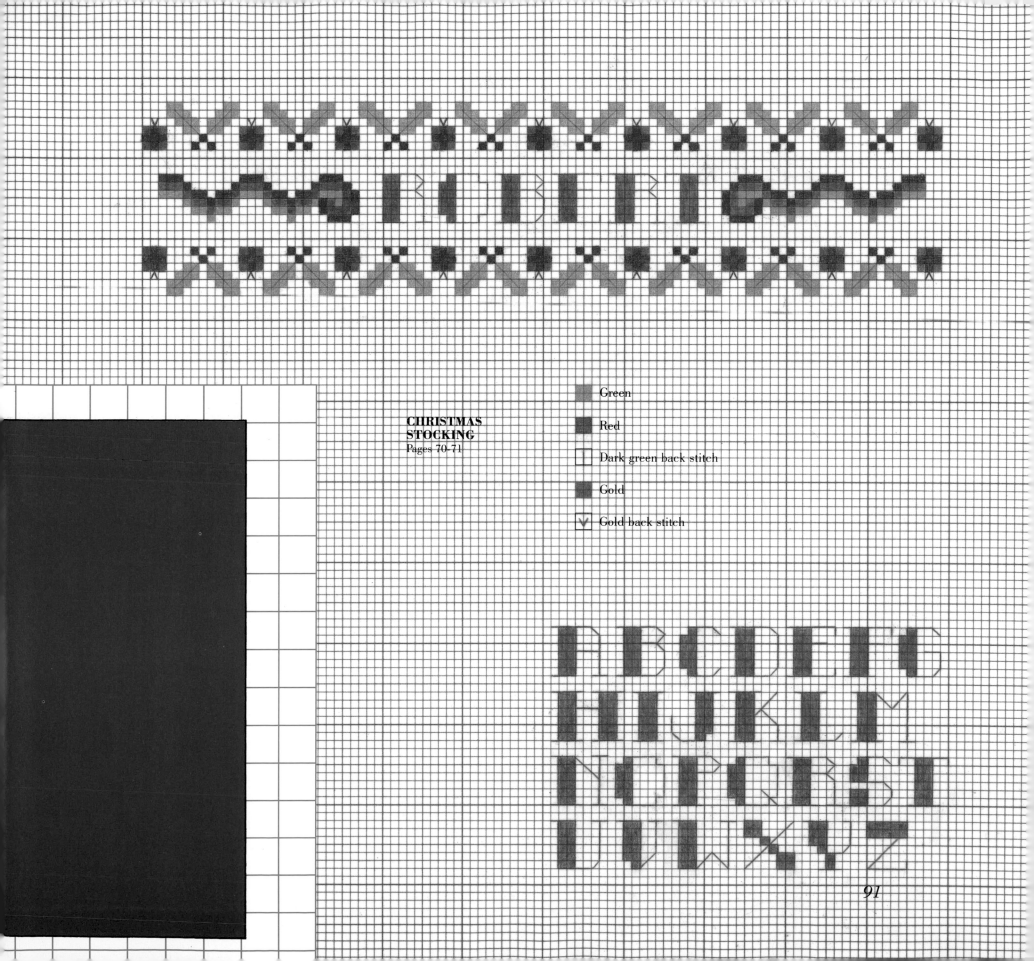

CHRISTMAS STOCKING
Pages 70-71

Green

Red

Dark green back stitch

Gold

Gold back stitch

ACKNOWLEDGEMENTS

The authors and publisher would like to thank the following:
DMC Creative World for supplying embroidery fabric and threads;
Framecraft Miniatures Ltd, 372-376 Summer Lane, Hockley,
Birmingham B19 3QA; The Handicraft Shop, Northgate,
Canterbury CT1 1BE for supplying various craft materials.

CREDITS

Contributors: Cheryl Owen pages 24-25, 34-35, 40-41, 48-51, 68-69;
Ming Veevers-Carter pages 26-27, 32-33, 38-39;
Anita Harrison pages 54-55, 66-67
Managing Editor: Jo Finnis
Editors: Adele Hayward; Geraldine Christy
Design: Phil Gorton; Nigel Duffield; Alison Jewell; Mary Hamlyn
Photography: Steve Tanner; Neil Sutherland; Peter Barry
Illustrations: Geoff Denney Associates; Phil Gorton; Richard Hawke
Typesetting: Mary Wray; Julie Smith
Production: Ruth Arthur; Sally Connolly; Neil Randles;
Karen Staff; Matthew Dale; Jonathan Tickner
Director of Production: Gerald Hughes